# BRIDGE
# THE LOVE GAP

**An essential guide to**

experience true love & connection in relationships

*Dear Asim (my chudhi buddy)*
*May love overflow in your*
*life. Thank you for all your*
*love and support. With love all*
*is possible*
*May you stay*
*blessed*
*Love & Light*
*Neela*
*— xxx —*

# NEELA GOHIL

**notion**press
.com

INDIA · SINGAPORE · MALAYSIA

# Notion Press

No.8, 3rd Cross Street,
CIT Colony, Mylapore,
Chennai, Tamil Nadu – 600004

First Published by Notion Press 2020
Copyright © Neela Gohil 2020
All Rights Reserved.

ISBN 978-1-63669-538-9

# Contents

# Preface

Bridge the Love Gap was written to serve you, to inspire you to move closer to discovering the real you. With so much uncertainty and ongoing change in the outside world, I believe it is essential to understand how to navigate through life with confidence and tap into love to build a bridge to connection and harmonious relationships. This book offers some essential tools to help you resolve conflict, communicate consciously and connect compassionately with yourself and others bringing about more happiness and harmony. It will guide you on a journey to a deeper understanding of love and relationships and show you how opening your heart is a pathway for expressing your authentic truth and living an 'inspiractional' life.

This book is dedicated for those people who are ready and committed to becoming the best version of themselves, to live life consciously, fully expressed and in alignment with their higher purpose. It will help you to experience true love and connection within yourself and in your relationships, and inspire your soul to take you to the next level of growth.

You will be guided to love more deeply, so you feel connected and radiate that inner self-love outwards, out into your close relationships and into the hearts of everyone you meet.

My name is Neela. I was born in Africa and have family roots in India, although I have been brought up and lived most of my life in the UK. I've studied the world of personal development and human behaviour in all its forms, which came about after having overcome my own emotional rollercoaster life journey and healing from a traumatic childhood which included losing my mother to cancer at a young age. I also witnessed the conflict and breakdown of my parent's relationship and, experienced my own health and relationship challenges. These experiences led me to learn and apply over 100 breakthrough modalities including hypnotherapy, NLP, Reiki, The Journey Method, Emotional Healing, and life coaching. It started an inner healing and transformational journey into self-care and self-love which deepened my understanding of the importance of love and connection in relationships and taught me how to relate better to myself and others.

I spent 15 years working in the corporate world, mostly in human resources within learning, leadership development and training. Here I saw how people behaved and handled relationship dynamics, and how they dealt with conflict and communication within the organisation as a whole and a team environment.

I've also had the freedom to travel worldwide over the last 20 years, including living and working in India for 7 years. India opened me up to love and deepened my spiritual growth and awakening journey further. It gave me a deep insight into a different culture and the challenges in love and relationships.

I have had the privilege of working with thousands of people from around the world of all ages, genders and backgrounds. I take a holistic approach in supporting my clients on an emotional, mental, physical and spiritual level through my coaching sessions and programmes. I also speak and serve at healing and personal development events whilst running my coaching, wellness and healing business.

My life's journey has been inspired by so many wonderful people, including my beloved mother (late Mrs Damyanti Gohil), who has been the inspiration for writing this book and the many friends, family, mentors, teachers and clients around the globe who I have had the pleasure to know, work with and learn from. I have combined all these experiences and learnings into this book. These people have been my guiding light for this work. Thank you for your energy and contribution to achieving my mission to touch the hearts and lives of millions, to inspire and empower people so that they break free of their barriers and transform. May this book help you to bridge the gap to creating more love, happiness, harmony and connection within yourselves and your relationships, so you live an 'inspiractional' life.

I now humbly dedicate this book with love to all the readers; may it help you discover the love that is within you.

# Acknowledgements

My deepest and heartfelt gratitude to all the souls that supported me in my journey to make this book and dream possible.

My parents, sister and brother

My family, soul family and friends

All my mentors and spiritual teachers around the world

School of Awakening – Sidra Jafri and the Awakening team

Brandon Bays

Arfeen Khan

My clients

The Creator

# Introduction

'If I accept the fact that my relationships are here to make me conscious, instead of happy, then my relationships become a wonderful self-mastery tool that keeps realigning me with my higher purpose for living.' – Eckhart Tolle

Are you someone who is in a relationship that has lost its 'spark' and want to experience more commitment, connection, love, joy, and intimacy?

Have you experienced past relationship challenges, been separated or divorced and want to learn how to re-connect and discover the true you?

Are you tired of being single and want to attract and desire an extraordinary loving, happy and harmonious relationship?

Whatever your current relationship status or desired outcome, congratulations for having the **courage** to take this first step on a **transformational journey** to **mastering love and connection.**

It won't always be an easy journey. There is no such thing as a 'perfect' person or a 'perfect' relationship. If you want real transformation and to experience lasting love, authentic relationships and live the life of your dreams, you need to be willing to look within yourself, to get some insight (inner sight) into discovering who you truly are and what matters most.

So, let me start by introducing myself and share some personal experiences and insights that have shaped who I am, led me on this journey and inspired me to empower others and write this book.

My life has been like a rollercoaster, full of ups and downs and unpredictability. In the early stages of my journey, when I was faced with countless problems, I became fearful and couldn't see the light at the end of the tunnel. Yet something was calling me into action, asking me to show up and trust the process of life despite the fear and uncertainty. I had to find a way out amidst all the chaos. I realised later that it is not the light that is the illusion; it was the tunnel that was the illusion and I needed to keep going through it to access the light.

Gradually I became accustomed to the constant changes of dealing with one thing after the other, which became the norm. I started viewing each problem instead as a challenge, looking for solutions to cross that bridge. I was guided to pause, to reflect and tap into a greater awareness, to listen and trust my inner gut, body, heart and soul. I believe we all are naturally intuitive; it is deep-seated within us, so we just need to learn to listen and quieten the noise that surrounds us externally and from within. This powerful gift of intuition, when used in the right way, will help you understand yourself better so that you can come into alignment and make better decisions in your life and relationships. I developed a natural instinct to live in the moment and trust what life was presenting to me. I made a decision to accept and move through the discomfort, to deepen my awareness and keep going no matter what.

I began to realise that life is a blessing and is happening for me, not to me, so I may as well enjoy it and not take it or myself too seriously. Nobody is given a handbook on life when they are born. We all learn from our experiences and understand how to live life the best we can from our level of awareness in that moment. Life would in fact be boring and predictable if we were told exactly what is to come next. As I tapped into a higher awareness and reflected on my past and the lessons it had offered, I stayed hopeful about how I could apply this to my future. As Steve Jobs says 'You cannot connect the dots looking forward, you can only connect them looking backwards. You have to trust that the dots will somehow connect in your future.' I had to trust that my soul has a plan, even if I couldn't see or make sense of it at the time. I had a deeper knowing that everything will unfold as it is meant to in perfect divine timing.

I now share how my story unfolded and the many lessons I learnt along the way, in the hope that it will inspire you to overcome any of your doubts or fears and empower you to bridge the love gap and live an 'inspiractional' life.

## What does 'inspiractional' mean?

Living an inspired life requires tapping into your truth, learning to tune into and trust your intuition to receive an inspired idea, focusing on it and then having the courage to take action. At the same time, you're working with spirit to guide you along the way. Writing this book is a good example of how I have taken inspired action and unleashed my creativity. I feel my soul has guided me all along, to come into flow and share my truth, despite facing many obstacles. It's been an ongoing journey of discovery right from setting the intention, through to connecting to my intuition and learning to follow the path of my heart's calling.

When you are living an inspiractional life, you feel like there is a fire within you (a spark); you are living life with a higher purpose. It's about growth and being of service and contributing to others. You can't wait to wake up every day. You feel grateful to be alive and motivated to make a difference. You live every day in greater awareness of yourself, and have a deeper connection to the divine, the universe, source, nature or something that is greater than yourself. Have you ever wondered what makes your heart beat, your eyes shine and your hair grow? It is the presence of that very consciousness that allows you to become present in each moment with yourself and others.

You start to become an observer of life; you watch your thoughts and notice how they impact the way you feel and behave. You tune into your body's wisdom and energy system for guidance. You come into harmony with your mind, heart and soul and start taking inspired action towards manifesting and creating your dreams. You feel lighter, happier and more loving.

## How the programming started

Our minds are being programmed daily. Either by the media, family, friends, teachers, doctors or your culture and society at large. This programming forms our beliefs early on in childhood, impacts our relationships, and literally everything we experience in the world. For example, if you watch a movie with a friend, you will both come away with a different interpretation and meaning of what it was about. We give meaning to life by perceiving information through our senses, what we see, hear and our feelings and we choose to filter out that which doesn't resonate for us. Your mind then creates stories based on your belief system and shapes your model of the world.

My childhood was traumatic, full of conflict and disharmony. I don't recall many happy memories and felt unsettled most of the time. I witnessed the breakdown of my parents' marriage, which was painful to see. My parents came from traditional Indian families, where marriages were arranged by the community elders rather than being done for love. My mother was married off by the time she turned 18 years old to someone she didn't know well, something I never understood. My parents had my sister, brother and I at a young age and my father did what he could to support the family. However, due to physical health challenges he was unable to work, so my mother became the main breadwinner. She worked tirelessly to make ends meet.

I remember from a young age seeing my parents struggle. There were constant arguments about money, bills, chores, and family which blew up out of proportion, ending in heated verbal exchanges and physical abuse. Yet through all these experiences I was taught humility, to appreciate everything and make the best of the little things in life.

My mother gave me a great deal of love and attention and made me feel safe growing up. As humans we all have different emotional needs. Some examples of these needs include a sense of belonging, connection, love, security, certainty or feeling accomplished. Everyone has their unique set of emotional needs, which derives from their upbringing, their identity and other individual factors. Children are usually more drawn to the parent who will satisfy and fulfil these needs, hence some have a stronger bond with one parent than the other.

At the heart of it, children just want to receive the gift of love, affection, and attention from their parents and others. They want to know they belong and feel safe in the world.

The most basic emotional human needs come from a theory in psychology developed by Abraham Maslow in 1943 known as Maslow's hierarchy of needs. In the 5 layers of the pyramid structure, Maslow's hierarchy shows the progression from 1) basic survival needs like food and water at the bottom of the pyramid, moving up towards 2) safety, through to 3) psychological needs of belongingness and love in intimate relationships, 4) esteem, respect and self-fulfilment needs through to 5) self-actualisation and achieving one's full potential at the top of the pyramid.

Now have a think about your childhood and upbringing. Who did you learn from? What did you learn from your parents or primary carers growing up? What were some of your emotional needs? How were these fulfilled or not fulfilled? Who gave you the most love or attention?

## My mother's love

'Love is blind; be careful', my mother used to tell me whilst I was growing up. At the time I didn't understand what she meant. Later, I realised that she was telling me when we are in love we only see the good things about the other person and we turn a blind eye to what we don't want to see. We get hurt. We become attached and addicted. We can lose ourselves in the process.

My mother's presence and energy would light up a room when she entered. She had a happy glow about her despite facing many challenges. Being very generous at heart, she spent her hard-earned wages, to make us happy first. She was abundant and loved life. Along with running the household, she took care of all the social engagements and managed to save up for special treats. She loved to serve, and uplifted others around her. It gave her immense joy to see others happy. In fact, she would often say 'This life, it only comes once; we come with nothing and go with nothing.' So she made the best out of everything. She had a great attitude to life.

Sadly though, my mother shockingly developed cancer when she was only 36 years old. It was the most unbelievable news which shook me to the core. She later got divorced as her health started to deteriorate. My mother was very strong-willed, yet after undergoing many invasive treatments, she passed away in August 1995 in her early 40's. She will forever be an example to me of an extraordinary woman, who was such a brave, kind and loving soul throughout.

This experience helped me to realise just how precious the people in our lives are. Life is short so it's important to resolve our inner and outer conflict which causes stress and can affect your wellbeing. I also learned that the love we receive from our parents or primary carers early on shapes our character; they are our role models as we grow into adults. Most importantly though, we learn from their belief system and the meaning they have given to life. We inherit these beliefs either consciously (with awareness) or subconsciously (where we are not fully aware).

Losing my mother opened me up to asking all kinds of deeper questions. I wanted to know why this had this happened. What is the meaning and purpose of life? What happens after death? I had so many unanswered questions and became hungry for the answers. Anyone who has lost a loved one or had a relationship breakup, can understand the pain, however each person deals with their emotions differently. Losing my mother was a tremendous loss, impacting my siblings and myself in different ways, yet it brought us closer together through the love we shared.

It taught me the importance of acknowledging and opening up to these strong emotions rather than pushing them away or numbing them out. Emotions are messengers from your soul. They are energy in motion and provide warnings that you need to address something. Yet, so many people choose not to listen to these messages, distracting themselves from their feelings, and later possibly manifesting some dis-ease within the body.

**"**

> What if there was a way to welcome emotions from a safe space, so that you can heal your heart from a space of love?

**"**

## The wake-up call

Looking after my mother was the main purpose of my life. After her passing, it left a huge gap of incompleteness. It was the wake-up call to explore myself, discover spirituality and live a more conscious life. Before that time, I had lived most of my life on auto-pilot, mostly unaware of my needs and reacting to circumstances. Supporting my siblings and focusing on my work initially bought some purpose into my life.

My awakening journey began as I started learning how to bridge the gap, becoming aware of life, embracing my feelings, asking for support and tapping into an inner strength of faith and possibilities.

## The pain of judgement

My father and I had parted ways when my parents got divorced. I didn't feel as emotionally connected to him and judged and blamed him for his behaviour. I was full of anger towards him. I couldn't understand or get through to him and wasn't in a good space. We became disconnected and didn't have much contact for almost 18 years!

I ignored and buried my feelings and carried on living life as normal. The subconscious mind is very powerful; it is a databank for everything that is not in your conscious mind. It stores your beliefs, your previous experiences and memories. Everything that you have seen, done or thought is there.

It has a way of reminding you that you need to deal with an issue. For a long time, just as I was falling asleep, I would see an image of my father, reminding me to deal with it. I would always send blessings and love, praying that these images would go away. Looking back, I now realise that holding onto the anger and resentment hurt me more; it left me with a restless feeling in the back of my mind and an uncomfortable feeling in my heart.

I discovered later on that we all need judgement in our lives to be able to function. Good judgement is when we use our discernment about a situation based on the facts and logical reasoning, and then come to a decision. The decisions we make in life also shape our destiny. Unfortunately, I had become blinded by the opinion of others and the circumstances; my emotions were high and had clouded my judgement.

Through healing myself, I became aware that not only had this judgement towards my father caused a lot of guilt and conflict within me, I had also judged myself. I became aware that love is the absence of judgement and that every time I pointed a finger of blame or judged others, there were three fingers pointing right back at me, asking me to take a deeper look at myself, to love and heal the wounded parts within.

Take a moment to reflect on how judgment has affected your decisions in your relationships. In which ways have you judged yourself and others in the past? Are there people in your life that you are still holding onto blame with? What if you could let it go? Thankfully, I discovered that there are tools and strategies that you can use that can help you to build a bridge of self-care and self-love and come into more acceptance and peace within.

## Relationship conditioning

Not forgiving my father earlier affected my relationships with men, as I attracted men with similar traits. For example, they became angry, used bad language, or became too controlling, possessive or were emotionally unavailable. However, I recognised this was a conditioned response and saw where this pattern was coming from.

Through much inner work, I understood how this unhealthful relationship with my father was the root cause of disharmony in my past relationships with men, and had created an internal barrier to love and connection.

Nobody had taught me about love, romance or relationships growing up. I didn't have any great role models to look up to and rarely met couples who were 'truly' happy or 'in love'. What did love even mean? In fact, I rarely opened up to anyone out of fear of being criticised and judged about my family situation. All I had seen was the struggle and pain in my parent's relationship. Society and mass media messages were loaded with fear and formed a subconscious negative imprint within me. This led to developing early relationship conditioning and inheriting some negative and disempowering beliefs about love, marriage, trust and relationships. On the other hand, I had also seen what love could look like from watching romantic Bollywood movies, which helped me to unwind and escape from reality for a while. It all looked like a wonderful dream of possibilities and happy endings.

People learn about love and relationships in many different ways, from observing others, watching movies or even listening to the lyrics of a song. How have you learned about love? What are your ideas of love? Who influenced you about love?

> **What if there was a way to clear any negative programming and learn how to love from a different level of consciousness?**

## Change starts within you!

It takes commitment and focus to do the inner work, to take 100% responsibility and be courageous in opening up your mind, heart and soul to building a bridge of love, compassion and connection towards yourself and others on all levels of your being.

Consider this for a moment; how much energy does it take to try and change someone? It's nearly impossible, wouldn't you agree? In fact, when you try to change someone, you may even be communicating to them that you do not respect or trust them. The change needs to come from within that person. When you stop trying to change others and focus instead on the only person you can change, (and that's you), then the transformation can begin. You'll notice everything comes into alignment and changes around you. It's surprising how everything else will just unfold and start falling into place, creating a ripple effect, to bring more happiness, harmony and love to all areas of your life.

## Relationships today

So why is it so important to focus on love and relationships now? Well, just take a look around you. Relationships are changing rapidly in these modern times. Are you aware that in most countries around the world today there is a significant increase in divorce rates and that figure is increasing daily? Almost 50% of marriages break down as there is no tolerance, happiness or fulfilment in the relationship. Society is also becoming more accepting of divorce and making it much easier to break out of relationships and move onto the next best thing. The number of domestic violence and mental health cases have risen too, as life challenges including financial situations, health etc., have led to increased levels of stress. Some even experience depression and contemplate suicide, feeling that they are unable to cope. In almost all these scenarios, the common factor to turn things around is receiving the right support, love and connection in relationships.

Through my observations and conversations with people around the world, the reality is that there are many more people who choose to stay single to avoid the challenges that being in relationships can bring; they fear losing their freedom or getting hurt, yet all the while deeply wanting connection and seeking out love.

> **What if you could be more conscious in your relationships and have the freedom to choose love?**

Whether you are in an intimate relationship, have deep friendships that are there for you or are on a spiritual path and connected to your higher self, I have come to believe that **relationships teach us so much about ourselves.** They are the necessary key to your source of happiness, truly discovering yourself, your growth, becoming more loving, connected and fulfilled. Without them, how could you possibly get to know yourself?

If you're not in a relationship currently, and want to be, aim to learn to become a better partner to yourself, so when the right person comes along you can support one another in a healthy way. Real growth should not be reliant on an external relationship alone. The focus needs to be on inner happiness and coming home to the real you.

When it comes to relationships and matters of the heart, there are many aspects and challenges that people are dealing with. However, most of the underlying issues are similar, regardless of gender, background or religion. Often, these challenges can become interlinked as we have different perspectives, experiences and values, and these can become sensitive issues to deal with.

This book highlights some of the most common issues and challenges I have come across through personal insights, experiences, research and working with clients from all backgrounds and in all areas of life. People often come to me with all sorts of issues including aches and physical symptoms or disease (backaches, stomach, cancer, etc.) or they're unable to shake off negative emotions and destructive reoccurring thought patterns. They often feel sad, lonely, anxious and overwhelmed or have a longing to attract their ideal relationship. The root cause usually relates to their love life or relationship with themselves and others. Deep down there is a gap, a craving for interaction, connection and a longing to feel alive, joyous and loved.

Let's face it relationships can be hard to deal with based on your personal life experiences, values and belief system, especially if you do not have the right support, tools or structure in place to guide you. The good news is you can learn to bridge the gap from wherever you are currently to where you would like to be.

## How important is your love life to you?

When you start a new career, you need the right guidance, tools, skills and ongoing coaching to be competent; the same applies to your love life and relationships. Despite it being important to many, it gets the least amount of attention and is the easiest to ignore. Do you take it for granted? How about thinking about your relationship as a hobby? Instead of thinking of it as being hard work, give it that attention, love and time it deserves.

Whether you are excited and happy about your love life or you are sad and lonely when things are not going well in your personal life, your love life affects everything else. Unfortunately, no one really taught us in school about love or relationships. We had to discover this on our own by trial and error and through our experiences out in the big wide world. Luckily, there are some conscious communities now that are bringing more awareness and light to these areas.

> **What if you could make your love life and relationships a priority?**

Let's go on to learn the reasons for the gap between where you are and where you want to be in your relationships and how to bridge the love gap to live the life you desire.

# Chapter 1

# What is the Love Gap?

———————— ∽∾ ————————

The love gap is the distance between your current reality of love in your relationships, (the conditions, beliefs and expectations) compared with where you would like it to be in your life. So many people feel unfulfilled as their blueprint of what they believe their life and relationships should be like doesn't match up to where they currently are, causing dissatisfaction. This gap can also be between the love we may have lost and the love we hope to find. It's in this gap where we learn to meet ourselves. Satisfaction comes when we learn to bridge the love gap and create a new blueprint.

Perhaps you are currently in an intimate relationship, married or dating someone. Things may look good on the surface; you may have the ideal home, kids, career, finances and material possessions. Yet deep down there is an emptiness, a gap, a deep yearning for more love, connection, intimacy and commitment.

Maybe you have come out of a relationship or are single, feel ready to meet a conscious partner, and want to learn some strategies to attract love in your life.

There are even people who may choose to go in and out of relationships for the sake of having connection. However, when you enter a relationship from a place of loneliness or boredom, you will be wasting precious time and could miss out on attracting the right partner.

**So how can your awareness of this love gap be used to move towards manifesting your dream life?**

Actually, the gap between where you are and where you want to be is full of possibilities, if you just take a moment to pause, to grace it with your presence and experience the wonder of it all. When you take the time to learn how to patiently love the gap, it can open you up to the hidden treasures that are waiting to be set free within; your intuition, creativity, and lifeforce.

## Appreciating the gap

You can work towards appreciating this gap. Fill it with the things that you love, things that inspire you to create connections; surround yourself with circles of people who bring the best out in you. At times, the people around you may continue to associate you with the person you used to be, a younger version of yourself. They may tell you that it's not you. For example, you were shy before and now you are becoming more confident. If this happens, become more of who you truly are and don't worry about what others think; it's all part of the process of transformation. Some will like you and some won't, and that's ok. As long as you accept yourself for who you are, and who you are becoming, you will begin to attract those people into your life who resonate with you.

To become the best version of yourself it's important to start working on your inner world – your mindset, beliefs, emotions, values and learning new skills or applying your talents to move towards your vision and purpose. **When things change inside you, your outer world begins to change**. This will involve self-acceptance, care and love. We tend to do more for others than we do for ourselves. Taking care of yourself is the kindest gift you can give to yourself on this journey. Some examples of self-care include giving yourself quality time and space to reflect, loving and pampering yourself, honouring your emotions, learning new things, resting, and getting to know yourself so that you can live a full expression of who you are. This can be hugely rewarding for your spirit and makes you feel good.

It's completely OK to be single and wait for the right person to come into your life as you continue to work on yourself, rather than being in a relationship with someone whose soul, energy and values are not aligned with yours. The only challenge you need to overcome here is letting go of any self-criticism and what other people think. Most importantly be kind and patient with yourself.

There's always more work that can be done to take you to your desired relationship state. Maybe you have repetitive thought patterns going through your mind, some past baggage that needs offloading, and are seeking answers to resolve your issues and feel understood. Do you want to learn how to become more conscious, to relate to another, to trust and feel deep love, to find real connection and a sense of purpose with yourself and others?

Everything you do starts with an intention. What is your intention for yourself? For example, 'I intend for my relationships be filled with more joy, love, kindness, and compassion' or 'I intend that my partner and I both feel deeply loved and supported by the other', or 'I intend to have a more meaningful connection with myself'.

Wherever you are, this book can guide you to bridge the gap to who you want to be and what you want to achieve. Writing down your insights in a journal will help you to reflect on the progression of your journey. Towards the end of the book, it will help you pull everything together to create your unique, **new Bridge Love Blueprint.**

## The wider the gap, the bigger the problem

I didn't want to repeat the same patterns as my parents, and it was possible that the example set by them may have turned me against wanting to be in a relationship. In fact, it was the total opposite. I had a deep desire to attract love into my life and manifested a wonderful partner. Initially we became good friends, dated and decided to get married later. I felt a genuine connection, he was supportive, had a good sense of humour and was kind. Knowing the qualities that are important to you in a relationship, can really help when it comes to deciding whether to take it to the next level. Also, developing those desired qualities within yourself will attract similar people into your life.

We came from different religions, which could have had consequences back then; it made no difference to us though, as we agreed that love should have no boundaries. I say this because there is still a bias towards people dating or marrying into the same culture, even in these modern times, mainly due to family reputation. Dating was fun and spontaneous for us, whilst marriage came with its many responsibilities. Our married life started well, yet the challenges and cracks started to slowly show up later and created a gap in the relationship.

Most of the problem lies in the **size of the gap**, whether you're single or in a relationship, looking for love, intimacy or a deeper meaning and spiritual connection, or have experienced some distance in your relationships which prevents you from feeling truly happy, connected or in harmony. Maybe deep down you feel alone, scared, rejected, betrayed or don't even know how to bridge that gap because being detached and isolated feels like a much safer option than committing to change, so day by day the gap increases without you even realising.

Have you ever felt this gap, this abyss, and emptiness inside, even though your life may look great to others on the outside?

If so, you are not alone. I experienced this emptiness when my marriage was on the rocks; **gradually the gap between us got bigger and bigger**. I loved and cared for my partner, and did my best to make things work to save the marriage. However, I couldn't make sense of what was going wrong. I kept asking myself, 'Why does this feel like such hard work? What have I done wrong?' It felt like an uphill struggle. I just wasn't equipped with the right support, knowledge or tools to break through my barriers to love and connection at that time.

From an intimacy and connection level, we went from being one of the most fun, playful, joyful and loving couples to hardly communicating.

The gap in romantic relationships often starts widening in your daily interactions. You go from sharing and doing mostly everything with each other to hardly saying hello. It slowly then reaches into the bedroom… you avoid eye contact and face away from each other and just lie there, enduring endless sleepless nights. Turning towards each other just feels awkward. Then the mind over-analyses, thinking up all sorts of things, replaying events and having unspoken conversations in your head. The pain gets unbearable. You don't dare to speak up or say what is really true for you. If you do speak it may end up getting into a heated argument, so you choose to remain silent. You eventually need to move away or sleep separately so that you have your own space, although those feelings of restlessness, tossing and turning, mind whirling remain until you eventually tire and fall asleep. Gradually, you barely even acknowledge or speak to one another, avoiding interaction and end up leaving the odd written post-it notes scattered around the home to communicate the things you need to say or chores that need to be taken care of in the hope the other will somehow acknowledge it.

The days just pass and turn into months with a secret hope that someday the situation will somehow magically get resolved.

In my case, communication between my husband and I had completely broken down. It was like living with a total stranger. We had grown apart and it scared the hell out of me. I kept asking myself, 'Where did the love go? How can I love him one moment and hate him the next? How and when did things get this bad? Why is this happening now? How long can I go on living like this?' It all happened so quickly. There were so many issues that started off small and eventually built up creating a brick wall between us. This wall grew stronger and taller each day. It felt out of control, creating a lot of confusion and anxiety. Neither of us had any solutions on how to break through the barriers. There was stubbornness, resentment, anger, a lack of attention, affection and appreciation on both sides. The gap was humungous! In the blink of an eye, we went from being happily married to it all being over.

Perhaps, some of the above sounds familiar to you? How have you experienced the gap? Learning how to bridge this gap through connection, communication and harmonising conflict can assist you in understanding yourself and others better, and take the stress out of your relationships.

## How do we bridge the love gap?

It was at that time that I realised I needed some time out, a moment of stillness to give my heart a chance to tell me where I really wanted to be.

This was the beginning of something new and led to me thinking differently. My search for a deeper truth began. I'm sure you've heard the saying, 'When the student is ready, the teacher appears.' Miraculously what I needed showed up at just the right moment, whether it was the right book, people, experiences or spiritual practices. I began to develop a deeper awareness and connection with my higher self, that part of me that is pure, all-loving and knowing, and to God, the source of love within and around me. My focus was on bridging the love gap, growing, creating a new beginning, a new identity and life.

The story above, and the one that follows, demonstrates some of the complexities in relationships that can spiral out of control and the consequences of not seeking out the right support or addressing issues in a timely manner.

---

### Bridging the love gap

I worked with a client who was under the care of her GP and 'labelled' with depression. Married for 14 years with 2 children, her marriage had lost its 'spark'. Her partner had stopped giving her any attention which led her to seek out an extramarital affair. She was no longer in touch with reality and used this to escape her issues of not feeling loved. She did not have the courage to express her feelings and thought she had found 'true love' in her new relationship, so walked out on her marriage. At first, everything about being together with her new lover was so thrilling and exciting, yet it later led to a pattern of co-dependency, addiction and lies that spiralled out of control.

---

The client came to me feeling full of disappointment, guilt and shame. She was confused, lonely and emotionally drained. Through our sessions together she realised that she had been living out an illusion in her mind regarding what 'true love' meant. She felt like true love had abandoned her which left her feeling vulnerable, having obsessive thoughts and feeling worthless. Unable to function at work, she was forced to leave her job and lost touch with her children and herself. She couldn't face anyone. Isolation set in, whilst she longed for intimacy, connection, and love.

As we worked together, the client was finally able to look herself in the mirror with eyes of compassion and accept the reflection for who she truly was beneath the pain. She courageously broke free of the inner barriers within herself, gaining clarity in her mind and body and re-balancing her emotions. She felt more content and connected within. She was empowered to express her truth to her partner, re-gaining love, respect, and trust with both him and her children. Most importantly, she gradually came off medication, resuming a state of good wellbeing and started to focus on her life and work. She finally bridged the gap of love within her heart.

## Relationship challenges – The 3 Cs

Within this book I identify three main themes that are considered to be the most common challenges in relationships. These are the 3 Cs:

1.  Conflict

2.  Connection

3.  Communication

Recognising and dealing with the 3 Cs is the solution to healing and overcoming most challenges. I will be sharing simple and practical solutions throughout the book to help you learn how to use these challenges to get the best out of your relationships.

## The 1st 'c' is conflict

What have you felt so strongly about that you've argued about it in the past? If you are in a relationship, this could be arguing about finances, chores, career, children, sex or not having enough quality time together. It can be a very stressful situation that causes constant conflict, resulting in mental and physical health issues.

It can leave you feeling drained and as if you've grown apart. There could be bouts of jealousy and resentfulness, acts of unfaithfulness, relationship break ups and possibly even divorce.

We all know that when you have arguments they're never really about the laundry or children. These are just the triggers, whilst the root cause of the issue goes much deeper than this.

If you are single, there may be some past baggage that you need to let go of or inner patterns of conflict that prevent you from gaining clarity and having harmony in your life.

**The Bridge to Love Method can help you identify the root cause, address the issues, heal and transform your life.**

So, let's take a look at the possible causes of conflict.

In the technological times we live in today, with the increase in digital communications, the number one thing that by far causes the most conflict in relationships is the inappropriate use of Facebook, WhatsApp, and all the numerous other social media networking platforms. The accessibility and freedom to connect with complete strangers and friends virtually from all around the globe is truly wonderful when utilised with the right intention. Just browsing and clicking on one button can bring you instant connection. However, for some relationships, this has been the major contributor to conflict, misunderstandings, feelings of insecurity, mistrust, infidelity and even break ups. It also leads to continued anxiety and addictive behaviour, perhaps secretly checking up on your partner's activity status and connections on their device to later use these as ammunition for a fight! So many people give more attention to their devices nowadays than their partners. I have also come across some couples who choose not to share their social media accounts to avoid any potential conflict or block one another when there is a disagreement.

Not having trust within your relationships can lead to unhealthy patterns of thinking and behaviour, such as feeling inadequate, comparing yourself to others, experiencing unhelpful emotions, mental stress, and physical pain. It prevents open communication, honest sharing, intimacy and joy, whilst robbing you of the love, commitment, and connection you truly desire.

**66**

> What if conflict has a purpose? What if it can be used to strengthen connection and empower yourself and the relationship?

**99**

## The 2nd 'c' is communication

One of the biggest challenges that causes conflict in relationships is the inability to communicate openly, not only in intimate relationships but in all relationships, whether with family members, work colleagues, neighbours or friends. In fact, it's essential to know how to communicate and behave in the world, how to relate to others, so that your needs are met and you can grow spiritually as a person. Not being able to communicate authentically limits you of your expression and suppresses your joy and spirit.

Have you ever felt that you were not being heard or understood? Do you find yourself shutting down mentally, withdrawing your energy physically, losing your voice or suppressing your emotions? Bad communication experiences can easily lead to not knowing how to express yourself from a place of compassion so that both partners feel understood, without feeling unloved, hurt or offended.

Loving expression is one of the most joyful, beneficial and healing experiences we can have in relationships and can enhance your life in all areas, and on all energetic levels: physically, mentally, emotionally and spiritually.

In this book client stories demonstrate how not communicating can harm your relationships, whilst purposeful communication and setting healthy boundaries builds trust and deepens relationships. Together we will look at simple ideas and solutions to help you communicate more consciously and lovingly whilst releasing unhealthy patterns that bring conflict and disharmony.

> **What if great communication starts with a recognition of one's own programming and patterns?**

## The 3rd 'c' is connection

The whole purpose of relationships and existence on this planet is connection. When we are born we need the utmost care, connection, protection, nurturing and love to survive. Connection is our life force to survival, even more so than love. When these basic human emotional needs are not met, we can experience many psychological and physical consequences that affect our wellbeing, life, and relationships later in adulthood.

### Where do you look for connection?

Rather than learning how to connect within, most of us look outside of ourselves to get emotional and physical connection, validation and love. This makes us feel better but can also lead to us staying in unhealthy relationships for fear of rejection. The same is true when we think we are missing someone; we are actually missing the connection of being aligned to ourselves. For many, love and connection are the number one emotional need that drives them at the core of their being, especially caregivers. We can end up invalidating ourselves, feeling depleted and putting a strain on the relationship if we do not bridge the missing connection to ourselves.

When interacting with various clients, my focus and intention is to enable and empower people to create a shift from looking to the outer world for connection and love to one of looking within to their inner world and being. This is where the journey to bridge the love gap begins, as to create the life and results we truly want, we must start to look within ourselves first, then examine our interaction with our lovers, partners, and within other relationships.

> 'What we experience in our outer world is a reflection of what is going on in our inner world.' – T. Harv Eker

We create our own realities. Many people experience low self-esteem, feelings of unworthiness and loneliness even when they are in a relationship or surrounded by others. This is because they don't have the desired internal awareness, connection, love and harmony. They spend so long looking at how to gain approval from others that they lose their own identity and sense of self in the process. Some people feel they are just biding their time, or are living on auto-pilot mode, especially those responsible for children or high career achievers. They work long hours and feel overwhelmed. They don't even make any effort to share quality time with each other, let alone themselves. They look towards their children or careers to give them the sense of gratification, achievement, and significance that is lacking in their lives.

Some couples end up losing interest in each other after the initial 'honeymoon period' wears off or take their partners for granted after being together for several years. They become set in their ways or even bored of the 'same old' routine and predictable conversations. They no longer feel an attraction towards one another. There is a disconnect to the desire they first felt towards each other versus their current reality. They feel they are not on the same wavelength. Their partner no longer understands them or takes an interest in their aspirations, dreams and fears. Not understanding their own or the other's vision, values and needs cause them to eventually drift apart.

"

**How would your relationship change if you felt connected to your partner at a deeper level?**

"

In the chapter Connection Bridge, you will learn the true meaning of connection and how to respect and understand each other's values to bring you much closer together.

Having coached many people who are single, they appear to have more freedom to do as they please, and can look like carefree, happy-go-lucky types. However, they often feel a longing desire to attract an ideal love partner to connect with or search for love endlessly, often attracting the wrong types of people, feeling disheartened and getting hurt. This has led to building walls around their hearts to protect themselves from feeling abandoned or rejected. They keep love out or become uncommitted, possibly even moving from one bad relationship to another. Whilst others make a conscious choice to stay single and want to deepen their connection with their higher selves. Many single parents that I have interviewed, say that they either don't have time for a relationship or may use their children as an excuse to not get into another relationship, to save any awkwardness or added complexities it could bring.

"

**What if you understood the energy of connection to add a deeper purpose and meaning to your life and relationships?**

"

People from all walks of life felt they had lost that spark, inspiration, and connection to themselves and others. They had conflict and commitment issues, experienced lack of communication, felt stressed and wanted more emotional connection, intimacy, compassion and love, but just didn't know where to begin. The same people discovered and used the practical insights and tools shared in this book to raise their awareness and created a new blueprint for love and life-enhancing relationships.

Most of you either have busy lives, or may have already done some personal development or inner work, so various simple exercises and tools are offered in each chapter that you can pick and choose from. The invitation is to make this a fun learning experience. Transformation can only happen as much as your psyche allows, with practicing and applying the tools eventually leading to them becoming a natural way of your being. It's been said it takes around 21 days of daily practice to create a new habit. Also, what you can measure is what you can improve upon. Take some time out to reflect after completing the exercises, so that you may notice how you are becoming more aligned, vibrant, joyous and bringing out your true authentic self in your relationships.

# Chapter 2

# Journey to Bridge the Love Gap

## What is love?

*'Love is the bridge between you and everything.' – Rumi*

There are a lot of different views out there on this big question of love. People have their own perception and meaning of the word based on their life experiences. It could be applied to the love of food, an animal, a child, your family, friends, partner or even God. In the context of romantic relationships, love is a complex variety of different mental and emotional states, beliefs and behaviours, which can make you feel affection for and connection with another.

Through conversations, some say that love is in the heart whilst others say it is in the mind; either the idea of love in their thoughts or an actual heartfelt experience. To add some clarity to this, did you know that we have a brain in the heart which has its own electrical system? Heartmath says that the heart is more powerful than the brain. They are in constant communication with each other, yet the heart sends more energetic information to the brain than it receives. Learning to be in unity with the qualities of heart energy helps you to experience more love and connection in your relationships. There are exercises later in the book to assist you to come into unity.

It's hard to define love without having a direct experience of it yourself. The moment we try to define love, that which is formless, we confine it to form. Let's take a look at the difference between spiritual love and being infatuated. Spiritual love is something that exists within you and around you and arises by your conscious choice. Love is how you feel emotionally inside. It is heartfelt. When you feel the love inside, everything outside of you reflects love. Love is not something that you do; it's already accessible within when you tap into your emotions, mindset, body and spirit. Love is present everywhere. It's the bridge between your mind and heart, body and soul, you and another, you and God. Love came before you were born and is here to stay. Infatuation on the other hand is usually a physical attraction or lust rather than love towards another. You feel the need for attention or to be comforted by the other. This can lead to co-dependency, or experiencing 'love-sickness' when that person is absent, and creates a disconnection with self, usually due to raised levels of cortisol, a stress hormone that has been shown to also suppress immune function. Then there is a love for food, for example chocolate. This is a different type of love. It's an enjoyment that may bring you the same internal feelings of comfort and being loved but it is only a temporary fix.

*When the mind falls in love, it's temporary. When the heart falls in love, it lasts a lifetime. When the soul falls in love, it's eternal.*

When you are on a journey to seek out love, how do you even know what you are looking for and how long it will take to reach? How do you know the difference between love at a soul level and love at a mental level and whether it is something you are missing or you want to re-connect to? Some people are more in love with the idea of love than love itself. They enjoy being showered with gifts or taken for candlelit dinners and may even need to hear the words 'I love you' as acknowledgment and confirmation that they're loved. Soul level love is eternal, a pure love and deeper spiritual connection to your being.

I believe that **love is always here**; we just lose sight of it when things are not going well. When some people say they 'fell out of love' with their partner, they are just expressing that they don't have the same feelings for their partner as when they first met. Their feelings and thoughts regarding love for that person have changed. How about thinking about love in another way? Instead of falling in love with someone or something, perhaps it's time to **rise in love** in all our interactions?

The way we experience love is personal according to how open to love we are. Take some time to reflect in your journal, and think about the following questions, so that you can establish where you are.

1.  What is your experience of love?

2.  How do you think and feel about love?

3.  What are you in love with?

## Love languages in relationships

When you first meet someone new and are in that initial dating phase, you do almost everything together and aim to impress each other. It's all about the way you look at each other, touch and talk to each other; all your needs are fully satisfied because you are so 'into' one another. You are full of love.

Then later, when the relationship dynamic shifts from dating to a more committed setup (like marriage or living together), you may not experience the same love from your partner, hence the question that arises time and again **'Do you love me?'** This usually comes into play when something feels like it's missing in the relationship. Expectations increase or you no longer receive the same acknowledgment from the other which creates a 'gap' in the relationship.

There are many ways that we express love. In fact, 5 types of love language have been identified by Gary Chapman, an American author. Whether it's physical touch, quality time, receiving gifts, acts of service or using words of affirmation. Discovering your love language and that of your partners will help resolve any mismatch in your communication. It will help you feel understood and rekindle love and connection again. More on how to understand these love languages in your relationship is covered in the chapter Connection Bridge.

## How do you know you are in love?

Romantic love can feel like a craving or an addiction for something. It can give you a feeling of butterflies in your stomach, skipping meals or restlessness when sleeping. When was the last time your heart skipped a beat as a result of being in love? You become distracted and all consumed by it. It's hard to stay present as you may daydream and fantasise about your experiences and feelings about the other in your head. It's like watching a great movie over and over again. The problem with new relationships though is that people often move too quickly. They overthink it and let their imagination run wild in their minds, figuring out how the relationship will look before even getting to know one another or committing to becoming exclusive. This infatuation leads to disappointment if the imagined ideas and expectations do not match up to the movie that has been created in their minds.

**Now take some time out to reflect in your journal about a time you have been in love and answer the following questions:**

- How did it make you feel?

- What were you thinking?

- What were you seeing?

- What were you saying to yourself?

- How did you experience life around you through the lens of love in terms of people, places, situations, etc?

## Love is the solution

*'The wound is the place where the light enters you.' – Rumi*

At the heart of it, we all just want to feel happy, connection and loved. We seek love in human relationships, and project our needs onto our partners, parents, family and friends in the hope they will complete us. Lack of experiences of love or past hurts can cause wounds that we carry deep inside us and can lead to self-destructive behaviour, addictions and negativity. **What if we can shine a light on these wounds?**

When we can accept these wounds with our full presence we can access love. Love meets every need in inconceivable ways. Love is eternal and has a powerful presence of being. Love is unconditional. Love was here before you came and will stay when you are gone. Love can melt the barriers in your heart and opens you up to gratitude, joy and bliss. Love is embracing, accepting, compassionate and forgiving. Love can heal and transform every being, every relationship, every situation, every problem, everything! Love is the solution. It seems simple, yet we make it complicated. **The greatest love that you can ever give another is the love you have for yourself.** When you pour that love from you onto others, you make the world a better place. Are you ready to awaken and open up to love?

*It's time to awaken and love yourself for all you have been through, all you are going through and all that you are becoming.*

## Spiritual journey of awakening to love

The spiritual journey of awakening to love can go through many stages depending on your life experience and your readiness. It often starts with feelings of emptiness or unhappiness, where you are experiencing some darkness or things may not look so pretty. This can be the entry point for you to look within and guide you to begin to shift your perception to seek answers and meaning. You may feel disillusionment or lost in the process, and this is very normal. Keep going. You are on the right track. **You need to be brave enough to explore the darkness that you discover and open into the infinite light and love within you.** When you are committed to doing the deeper work, the journey within leads you to finding those answers, experiencing insights and breakthroughs along the way. The universe comes in to support you, guiding you to the right tools and connecting you with light-minded people. You integrate your learnings and come into a space of love, joy and expansion. **You become the beauty and strength that arise after darkness.**

43

### Awakening to love

Through my awakening journey, I faced countless wounds head-on and connected to my intuition. Giving myself permission to welcome and shine a light on the dark places within and embrace them gently really helped me to open up and allow all emotions to flow freely without judgement.

My first direct experience of unconditional love was when I was sitting quietly in meditation. I felt what I could only describe as a tingling energy radiating out from my heart that gently filled my whole body. There was an expansion into lightness, a feeling of indescribable stillness and warmth into the very essence of my being. It was hard to move. I felt peaceful in my mind and body. In that moment, I merged into a oneness, feeling connected and embraced by something greater than myself. Love was present all around me. It brought tears of gratitude to my eyes, connected to the love that I had been seeking; it had been so close, within me all along. It felt like the purest form of 'being love'. I could feel, hear and see love in everything around me, and felt truly alive.

I have since kept up my meditation practice daily, with no expectations of re-creating the same experience. I learned that which comes also goes, to let it come and go. I am still a work in progress. Clearing any negative emotions first also brought alignment, clarity and deepened the practice. Meditation has brought me much closer to myself and taught me to embody my awakened self. It has increased my awareness, bringing more harmony and appreciation to everything in my life. This gratitude brings me into a state of love.

## Why does love hurt?

*'Love is the only thing in this world that does not hurt.' – Liam Neeson*

It's the painful feelings of loneliness, rejection, and losing someone that hurts. Love itself doesn't hurt. Pain is a part of life and we all experience it at some time. I believe we do not need to cover up our pain. Rather than turning away or covering it up we need to acknowledge it, release any negative emotions and memories, learn from them and open ourselves up to a love that makes us feel wonderful again. Love is the source of who you are. In fact, we learn more about ourselves from painful experiences at the end of a relationship, than at the beginning.

## Why do we need relationships?

*'I don't think that anything happens by coincidence... No one is here by accident... Everyone who crosses our path has a message for us. Otherwise they would have taken another path, or left earlier or later. The fact that these people are here means that they are here for some reason.' – James Redfield*

We meet people in the most unexpected ways. I believe loving relationships and connection are the key source to happiness, whether with a romantic partner, through deep friendships or with some greater source such as nature or your higher self. We encounter relationships with everyone we meet, and every relationship is just a key into the doorway of our own being and a meeting of ourselves. When we can learn to befriend ourselves, we can feel complete within.

Through researching a variety of relationship trends and studies published, I came across some findings published in The Lancet, a leading science journal. According to their findings a monumental decline is expected in the number of births over the next hundred years, which could see nearly every country's population shrinking by the end of the century, with as many people turning 80 as there are being born by 2100.

With the declining birth rates and the increase of non-committed relationships, here is a summary in my opinion of why I think it is important to become more consciously aware of what we are creating.

If the current relationship trends continue around the world we can almost certainly predict the future. As we entertain fake relationships or become addicted to non-committed dating, the love gap will widen and relationships will just become about having physical intimacy without love. Long distance and virtual relationships are on the increase too.

With birth rates continuing to decline, there is less commitment to entering into relationships or marriages for the purpose of co-creation and instead co-habitation which will influence future generations. With the increase in divorce rates and breakups, especially for those who have children or are single parents, the future of their children will be greatly impacted.

Relationships act like mirrors, they reflect back who you are and can help you see what you like and don't like about yourself. It's been said that you don't need to go to India to find a guru. Your partner/ friend/ family member is your guru and becomes that mirror! They are a blessing in disguise, even though it may feel uncomfortable at times. What can you learn from them? How often have you looked into the mirror to appreciate what you see?

Relationships can be challenging and uncover the parts of you where you feel vulnerable, disconnected, and unloved. Equally, they can bring about a wonderful sense of joy and upliftment and allow you to see the best of you. When you feel totally comfortable being in your own skin, you can bring your true authentic self into a relationship; you value it more and it can strengthen your spirit and growth. There is an increase in your levels of happiness, your health improves, and you feel on purpose. It's therefore vitally important you have good quality relationships.

> 'The quality of your relationship determines the quality of your life.' – Esther Perel

The quality of your relationships can either inspire you into action or hold you back. Maybe you value someone who is disciplined and proactive in achieving their dreams, behaves with confidence, has amazing energy, or a great attitude to life and the way they embrace challenges.

**Exercise: Valuing relationships**

Now list the three relationships that you value the most. It could be a significant other, a family member or friend.

1. What is it specifically that you value most about them?

2. Which of their qualities would you like to embody in yourself?

3. What are the most important qualities for you to have a happy relationship?

4. How would having these qualities impact the quality of your relationships and life?

## What do you need in love?

Relationships are formed on different levels to fulfil different human needs (psychological, emotional, physical, financial or social needs).

We all have different needs and desires in love when we look at it from the **4 dimensions of energy.**

**At the mental level,** it could be your ideas and thoughts of love. You'd like someone to say certain words or buy you gifts to make you feel loved.

**At the physical level,** to fulfil a desire for sexual connection, to be adored and be touched with affection through being intimate, i.e. hugs, kisses, gestures or massage.

**At an emotional level,** to connect with compassion, communicate your feelings with another, to share your problems and have meaningful conversations, feel heard and understood.

**At a spiritual level,** to have a sense of meaning and purpose in your life, to connect with something higher, such as God.

With so many expectations of love though, no one person can possibly fulfil all your needs.

These human needs and desires have arisen because people feel incomplete, yet want to experience feeling complete within themselves. Relationships help to fulfil this longing for love and connection.

It's easy to be joyful when everything is going well in your life. When you are happy, everyone seems to look beautiful and relationships improve. When you experience pain and negativity or things are not working out the way you hoped, you start to perceive the world as a dark place and no longer feel the passion inside to work on your relationships. That's when you may start to become depressed.

Some people seek out a relationship just to fulfil their needs to become happy. This, however, is only a temporary fix to happiness as it comes from a place of neediness. **The purpose of the relationship is to get to know yourself using the other person as a mirror, to reflect the areas you need to work on and grow.** This can be achieved by learning to become aware of your needs, behaviours and patterns. You then become more open and receptive to what the relationship is teaching you. In order to experience a fulfilling relationship, you must dedicate the time and energy to invest in the relationship, your own personal development and growth. Staying open to feedback and learning to communicate for understanding and connection is key to the growth process.

### Looking for love in the wrong places

Sarah was a lady in her late forties. She felt lonely and wanted to attract love. When I asked her what she really wanted out of life or loved to do, she always said she didn't know. She worked tirelessly doing work she didn't enjoy. Her parents had passed on and she hardly kept in touch with her only sibling. She had many old friends and would go out of her way to see them, yet she didn't enjoy their company as they would judge and criticise her lifestyle. She also attracted men who were emotionally unavailable and found herself taking care of them instead of being supported by them. She was anxious and suffered insomnia which made her feel tired.

I could see how her not spending time with what made her truly happy and her desire for love and connection, from a place of loneliness resulted in her choosing the wrong type of men. As we broke through her negative patterns, she discovered how not being aligned with her needs and her environment had led her to look for love in the wrong places.

Sarah was finally able to let go of these unhealthy relationships by saying no to them and so saying yes to herself. It took patience, practicing self-care, and compassion for herself. For a while she felt a void. However, it filled up quickly with love as she began to feel connected and accept herself. She reconnected with her sibling and attracted new opportunities both at work and in her personal life. She met people who were more aligned with her emotional needs, and felt more energetic, joyful and alive.

## The secret to love

*'Only in relationship can you know yourself, not in abstraction, and certainly not in isolation.' – J. Krishnamurthy*

Relationships teach us how to love ourselves. Without a relationship, how would we possibly discover who we truly are? It's through relationships that we find that the secret to love is being happy within. Most people get confused between being happy and being in love. **When we focus on being happy first, we can then bring that happiness into our relationships** and all areas of our lives. We have the power and choice to be happy in any given moment.

I have frequently visited Dharamshala in India, the home of the beloved Dalai Lama who is the spiritual leader of Tibetan Buddhism, which teaches compassion and happiness. I have spent sacred time walking in silence, soaking up the scenery and mountain air, quietly observing nature and the monks interacting with life. I was curious to know how a monk, sitting in his cave or on a mountain top in solitude, could possibly understand relationships. This kind of solitude can be blissful, yet it is through interacting with others and life that you truly learn about yourself and relationships. Taking quiet time out for yourself can be really beneficial, however, no matter which path you choose to take, coming into alignment with your being first will bring a better understanding of who you are and transform how you interact with others.

My curiosity led me to speak to some Buddhist monks and so learn more about their perspective on relationships, happiness and love.

### The monk's perspective on happiness and love

One of the monks kindly shared that he believed it was his destiny to gain knowledge and wisdom through working on his mindset using Buddhist teachings, which enabled him to be a better person and serve humanity. To do this, he had to practice self-care and became completely focused on mastering his mindset and his mission to serve the Dalai Lama, people and country.

For other monks, the Lord Buddha's teachings taught them to give up on the attachments which had caused suffering and internal conflict earlier in life. Practicing these Buddhist teachings daily helped them become unconditionally loving and harmonious. It enabled them to master themselves and practice compassion, not from a place of detachment, but one of inclusiveness and acceptance of others within the community.

Therefore, the desire for an intimate, physical connection to another didn't resonate with them, as they were consciously aware of the true connection to self and the source of all being.

A gifted spiritual teacher I had the privilege to meet was Nithya Shanti, a Buddhist monk for 6 years, after which he was guided to live and serve in broader ways than the traditional role of a monk permitted. I have attended many of his teachings. He is in a romantic relationship now which has opened him up to continue learning more about himself and others. He shares his relationship journey with passion and spreads joy with everyone he meets.

There are also a few former monks who are now famous such as Robin Sharma and Jay Shetty who have also demonstrated that following the spiritual path and practicing the art of mindfulness has enabled them to create wonderful conscious loving relationships, serve and live with purpose.

## How can I find love?

*'Your task is not to seek for love, but merely to seek and find all the barriers within yourself that you have built against it.' – Rumi*

As the quote above says, the way to find love is to look within yourself and to breakdown the inner barriers that are stopping you. So, the questions to ask yourself are, what will that love give you when you get it? How will love change your life? Are you willing to seek the barriers within and release the patterns that stop you? **What if there was a way to connect to the love that is already inside of you, instead of seeking externally to find it?** It's a gradual process. There are exercises later in the book that will guide you to self-love and look internally for this purpose.

## How can I get into a relationship?

Some of my clients are rather shy or too nervous to go out to meet new people. They prefer to attract a relationship in organic ways, through introduction from family or friends. Others feel confident to experiment with the online dating space and have had success. Yet both types may face issues with the fear of being rejected. There are many ways of dealing with rejection, from sharing your experiences with someone and feeling your emotions. The best way to deal with rejection is to work on your self-esteem and move forward again. When you respect and value who you are, and intend to enter a relationship with an openness to learning about yourself and growing together, it can be a truly wonderful experience. Most of all, rejection is not who you are. It is an emotion that stems from a belief system, which can be easily cleared.

Whether we choose to meet someone face to face or online, the key thing here is to focus on being authentic and in a great state. Did you know that it only takes around 7-20 seconds for someone to form an impression of you when they first meet you? This may sound simple but means you should consider a few things. Firstly, when dating, you want to look the part, so dress up for the occasion, yet be comfortable. Your choice of clothes and colours reflects your personality and style, plus it will make you feel good. Naturally, you may be nervous. However, smiling, even if it's when speaking over the phone, upgrades your voice tonality and how you come across, so will ensure you make a lasting impression. Your energy levels and mood are key here. Maintain open body language, be mindful of your posture and remember to make good eye contact; it shows you are curious, listening and connected. Be your natural self. There's no need to try to be someone else. Let your quirkiness and playful side come out as it creates attraction. Maintain the conversation by sharing interesting stories. Having a sense of humour will also help to build connection and increase your confidence. Remember though, you needn't share your whole life with them in the first interaction; take time to build up rapport.

If you decide to try online dating, do so in a conscious manner. Remember to be human despite the digital interaction. Find out as much as possible about the other person, not just by looking into their social profile, but by actually connecting with them, whether through a conversation over the phone or on a video call. The same skills of listening for connection and being natural apply here. If you are communicating in written form, ask meaningful questions and add some playfulness. Let the conversation flow. Then take the next step of meeting up when it feels right for both of you. The upsides of an online space are that it allows you to accept or refuse someone quickly, so there is less time required.

Meeting people in person gives you more insight about your compatibility. Proximity to another creates more chemistry, increases attraction and determines whether you have real connection over time. There is no wrong or right answer. When your vibration is high, you will more likely attract and manifest love organically; it often happens when you are least expecting it.

The most important thing to remember about getting into a relationship is to know yourself before walking into one; it will save you a lot of time. **Find yourself before you find another!**

## Letting go to manifest

The most successful relationships are those where two people know themselves; they know what they want and don't rely on the other to complete them, instead supporting and growing with one another. They let go of their expectations, beliefs, situations or people from their past before manifesting what they want.

---

### Shutting the door on the past

A client in London had gone through a painful divorce and stayed single afterwards for many years. Her heart desired to find love again and she made multiple attempts to meet new people and start dating. However, she didn't resonate with any of her dates and couldn't see a future with any of them, leading to her feeling disheartened. Through our coaching sessions, I could see that her thought patterns had led to her sabotaging future relationships as a result of the emotional attachment she was still carrying. Although she thought she had moved on, she was replaying the negative beliefs at a subconscious level of 'I'm not deserving of love' and 'nobody will be good enough for me' which had been created in her previous relationship. Once she became consciously aware that she wasn't finding the right partner because she hadn't allowed herself to get closure from her past relationship, she was finally able to let go and fully shut the door on her past, allowing her to feel free.

---

Within a matter of weeks, she met someone who just happened to work in the same building. Their friendship felt easy as they began to get to know one another and deepen their connection. Soon after I received a call saying they had decided to move in together and within a year I heard they had got married and were very happy together and planning to start a family.

There are many such stories like this of people who have met their ideal partner through work or living in the same building. If you are destined to be together, the universe will lead you to find one another. Around 60% of people meet their partners through a mutual friend.

At the same time, it's also a good idea to reflect upon what your interests are and where the kind of man or woman you want to be with likely spends their time. Remember opposites attract and you may not necessarily meet them in the bar. You could try going with an open mind to a place which lends itself to a hobby or interest of yours, i.e. a book club, yoga class, park, coffee shops, the gym, meetup groups. This way you'll meet people with a shared interest, which could lead on to the relationship you desire. It's all about having that confidence to move forward.

**Can I be best friends with my ex?**

You simply cannot be best friends with the person you just broke up with. It takes some time. You can eventually be connected as friends, just not on a daily basis and should avoid making it a habit and getting into the trap of things being 'normal'. First you should clear any negative baggage from when you were in that relationship by giving yourself some much-needed space and time to do so. The 'no contact' rule works for any length of a relationship. Ensure you avoid playing games with yourself and your former partner, so you can create respect in your relationship and all areas of your life. When we are respected, people want to be liked by us and that's powerful.

After a breakup, why not find other people to connect with? Now, I'm not suggesting you get into another relationship too soon! This is just about connecting with people other than your ex-partner as you do your inner work and cut your ties in a healthy way. In the long term, you can be friends if you choose to do so, when you have both moved on and the emotions are healed.

If you do want to become friends again at a later point, ask yourself 'What is my intention for being friends?' There may be a soulmate connection that brings that person back into your life naturally. The real test to whether you have moved on from a relationship is how you would feel if you were to bump into your ex-partner. Are you confident, strong and centred in your being?

It can be hugely traumatic when you break up with someone and it's not unheard of to get back together with an ex-partner. It may be thrilling, exciting and fun initially, but it will only last if you truly resolve the deeper issues.

Whatever the circumstances you find yourself in, know that putting in the inner work and getting through a breakup will make you powerful and give you a breakthrough.

---

### Why do I keep attracting the wrong relationship?

Mina kept attracting relationships where she felt controlled by men. She felt uncomfortable, as if she were 'walking on eggshells around them'. She loved them so tolerated their controlling behaviour, yet was unable to express herself and would often feel under personal attack. This meant she was unable to stay in a relationship for long and would walk away. She felt guilty about this, even though she felt she hadn't done anything wrong.

Our sessions empowered Mina to uncover her disempowering beliefs about men which rooted back to her controlling father. She cleared all these traumatic memories on a cellular level and came to forgive herself and her past, simultaneously creating new empowering beliefs about men. She started attracting better suited men, became more expressive and emotionally empowered. She now experiences the gift of being in a relationship with ease, free and comfortable in her own skin.

Are you willing to overcome your relationship challenges and learn the lessons they have to offer? If so, it will allow you to discover your true essence, to become conscious and live your life with passion and purpose.

The secret of a beautiful relationship is to become more conscious and learn to focus on enhancing yourself on all levels – mentally, physically, emotionally and spiritually. The key factor to feeling happy and fulfilled is the quality of all your relationships, whether with family, friends, professionals or on an intimate level. Always look towards understanding and meeting your needs and the needs of others, instead of trying to fix, control or manage them.

## Love exists

*Love exists when you believe in it, goes stronger when you trust in it and lasts if you have faith in it.*

A true relationship is where you **accept the past, support your present and encourage your future**. Certain people come into our lives for a reason, a season or a lifetime to teach us the lessons we need at just the right time so we can grow and evolve. There are no coincidences. The people you meet are either reflections of a repeated cycle or guides to a new start. Notice the difference. Can you think of such people who have entered your life? What have they taught you? Similarly, are there relationships you have entered and become someone's reason, season or lifetime? What have you taught them?

## The gifts of relationship – Soul lessons

As I look back, I realise these relationship challenges brought me the best possible gifts and were a wonderful blessing in disguise. I wouldn't wish to change any of them. I've since realised that we come here as souls to the physical world, having made prior contracts with certain people to teach us specific lessons in this lifetime. These souls cross our paths in this life at a certain period, to help us complete these karmic lessons and evolve. It's up to each one of us to learn the lessons, otherwise they just continue from lifetime to lifetime. We are not only here to learn karmic lessons though; **we are here to create and express ourselves as love.**

These experiences taught me many lessons including self-love and a connection to a deeper truth and way of being. I have completely healed from my past relationships by applying the knowledge and tools learned. I have a different level of understanding and meaningful connection with my ex-husband. I'm finally open to feeling the love from my father and understand men and their purpose in my life. I now experience authentic and open-hearted connections with people all around the world. There is much more appreciation, happiness and love in my life.

I've devoted most of my time and energy to discovering how to heal, to love and transform in relationships. **This journey has led me to discover and create a breakthrough Bridge to Love Method, a roadmap to bridge the gap, which I would like to share with you in the next chapter. I truly believe that love exists and can inspire you into action so you too can live an inspiractional life!**

# Chapter 3

# Awareness Bridge

―――――⌒∽⌒―――――

## The Bridge to Love Method

**The Bridge to Love Method** is a step by step roadmap to bridge the gap and guide you to create your own **Bridge Love Blueprint**. The Method will empower you to transform yourself and create lasting love, connection, joy and harmony in relationships.

The method is based on direct experience, application and breakthrough success stories of people I have had the privilege to work with. It covers specific processes, daily practices, tools and experiential activities that will enable you to **Bridge the Love Gap**. By overcoming your challenges, you will re-ignite the spark of joy, passion, trust and intimacy, so that you experience more deeply fulfilling relationships, feel alive, happy, loving and have a heartfelt connection with yourself and others.

**The Bridge to Love Method** is based upon a common coaching methodology which is used widely to assist with transforming beliefs, values, thoughts, feelings and actions to results.

```
          ▲
      ┌─────────┐
      │ Results │
      ├─────────┤
      │ Actions │
      ├─────────┤
      │ Feelings│
      ├─────────┤
      │Thoughts │
      ├─────────┤
      │ Values  │
      ├─────────┤
      │ Beliefs │
      └─────────┘
```

Starting at the bottom of the pyramid, our **beliefs and values** influence our **thoughts** and decisions. These are at the core of who you are and what is important to you.

Our **thoughts**, the mental doubts, stories, illusions that we tell ourselves and others, affect the way we **feel.**

Our **feelings,** and the chemical release in the brain of serotonin, dopamine and adrenalin, impact our physical body, **behaviours** and the **actions** we take.

Our **behaviours and actions** and the way we react to circumstances and events develop our character traits. **These actions then become the results we create in our life.**

**In summary, what you think and feel is what you create!**

It may seem simple, yet takes conscious awareness of all areas and commitment to put this into practice and action, to truly achieve the desired outcome and results. Outlined below is the 7-step roadmap for bridging the love gap. More detailed information is covered under each step in the chapters that follow.

## 7 Step Breakthrough Bridge the Love Gap Method and Roadmap

**Step 1: Awareness Bridge** – we work on **discovering your truth** assessing where you are currently in your relationship and life using the **Triple 'A' Bridge Formula.** This raises awareness, acceptance and action so that you achieve more **clarity** and **focus** on what you want.

**Step 2: Mindset Bridge** – you will learn some powerful tools to **master your mindset and thoughts** so that you feel more focused, **gain clarity** to make **better decisions** and have **peace of mind** in your relationships.

**Step 3: Heart Bridge** – you will learn how to **master your emotions and connect with the heart of who you truly are** so that you can **powerfully express** yourself and come into **alignment.**

**Step 4: Harmony Bridge** – you will learn how to **bridge the barriers to conflict** and deal with stress, understand your **behaviour** and **expand on a physical level** to **create more harmony**, love and peace in your relationships.

**Step 5: Communication Bridge** – you will learn how to **communicate with courage and compassion** so that you can **impact and influence others** to feel understood and **get what you need** from your relationships.

**Step 6: Connection Bridge** – you will learn how to **connect for deeper meaning and purpose** within yourself and with others so that you **build intimacy and trust** and never have to feel lonely again.

**Step 7: Self Love Bridge** – you will learn how to tap into your **energy body** to **love** and **care for yourself** through **acceptance** and **forgiveness**, so that you experience more **compassion** and **gratitude** and **become loving** in your relationships.

**Outcome: Bridge Love Blueprint** – **breakthrough to feeling more love, confident, happy and fulfilled.** You become a magnet for **attracting love**, your relationships improve and you **manifest wonderful experiences** into your life. **You become inspired with love!**

## Triple 'A' Bridge Formula

### Step 1: Awareness Bridge

The first step in the **Bridge to Love Method** is the **Triple 'A' Bridge Formula**, the beginning of transformation, which will give you more awareness, clarity and focus on the journey.

> *'Awareness is like the sun, when it shines on things, they are transformed.' – Thich Nhat Hanh*

How would you know what needs to transform if you do not have any awareness of it? Most people have little awareness about themselves, their situation or clarity on where they are headed until someone else points it out; it's often a blind spot. The **discovery sessions** I've conducted with people have given them more clarity about themselves and the areas they need to work on in their relationships. It's not that people don't care about or love one another. They may just have a lack of self-awareness about their 'inner' world which causes disconnection within themselves and with others. When we experience more awareness, we become empowered to make changes and can identify what needs improvement through building on our strengths and areas for development.

Regardless of your relationship status, whether you're just starting out, or you've been working on transforming it to the next level, or you want to deepen the connection you have with yourself, there are steps you can take which will prepare you for harmonious and happy relationships.

**The first step to bridging the gap is to become aware and discover your truth, to assess who, and where you are now in your life and your relationship journey and where you want to be.**

---

### Exercise: Discovering your truth

Please take some time to answer the following questions:

1. Where are you currently in your life and relationship?
2. What do you love about yourself?
3. What do you want from your relationship or a future relationship?
4. What is preventing you from taking your relationship and life to the next level?

   **If you have a partner...**

5. What is the reason you got into this relationship in the first place?
6. What does the relationship give you?
7. What effect does the relationship have on your day-to-day wellbeing?
8. How does the relationship make you feel generally?

---

Now think about your situation and reflect on the following scenarios:

The best relationships are those where you are both committed to doing whatever it takes to make the relationship work, to apply the tools and develop yourself.

There are many different types of relationships. Maybe you understand the relationship on a **mental level** and logically know what works and what doesn't, and what must be done to create a better relationship, but you are not taking any action or feeling it. This is because there is a mismatch between your mind and heart. You are blocked somewhere.

Perhaps you are in a relationship where there is love, but your partner is not there for you emotionally or physically, whether you have children together or not. Maybe you feel that connection most of the time, but notice that when it's not present, things fall apart. This can be especially hard to manage for those in long distance relationships with the added challenge of being apart. For you to grow together, you must learn how to sustain this connection on a daily basis to keep the love alive, otherwise it just won't work.

Perhaps you are single and a high achiever in other areas of your life, yet feel lonely in your own company and want to experience a deeper connection with yourself and others, or want to attract a new relationship.

Maybe you have become accustomed to a standard routine and the different roles you both play, yet if something were to happen unexpectedly you wouldn't know how to manage. These patterns become habits that get wired in your brain. For example, getting up and going to bed at the same time each day or having the same breakfast and set meals in a week.

Start to notice your daily patterns and don't take anything for granted. I'm not saying that routine is a bad thing here, but sometimes it can stifle you. Be prepared for change and spontaneity! For example, one of you may suddenly lose your job or develop a health condition and the roles in your relationship may become reversed.

Think carefully for a moment about how this could apply to your current reality and write down the answers to the following questions:

1. *What is the current problem/issue?*

2. *What is your mindset and thinking about the situation?*

3. *How do you feel about it?*

4. *What is your vision for the future?*

5. *Who do you want to become?*

---

### 3 elements in relationship

A male client shared that the reason he wanted to get married was that he had a desire to have a child together with his wife. As soon as the child was born the intimacy ceased within the relationship. Sure, the child brought them closer in the beginning, but the focus was on the child so the relationship between them was neglected. Neither of them were getting their emotional or physical needs met. We had a session where he received more clarity about the reason for entering into the relationship. This led him to have an open conversation with his wife. The biggest realisation was they had forgotten that there are 3 elements in a relationship: 1) there is you as individuals, 2) there is your partner and then 3) the relationship itself. Once they had this awareness they were able to bridge connection and rebuild intimacy.

---

## Getting to the heart of your why?

Knowing what you want in life is critical; you may not always get what you want though. A guru once told me that God gives you what you need, not what you want, as he considers what's best for your growth. However, it's natural that we all still have wants and desires so it's a good idea to focus on them instead of denying yourself or regretting it later.

When asking people what they want they usually tell me they don't know. This just comes from a place of fear and is the minds way of keeping them safe. When probing further and using a little imagination, they usually come up with something. If fear comes up whilst doing this, know it's normal; shift your focus to the opposite of that, whether it is faith, love, happiness. Once you decide what you want, knowing your why is vitally important to give you the emotional stamina and 'inspiraction' to move towards it and create a vision to succeed with more certainty.

### Exercise: 7 levels deep

Getting to the heart of your why will create a deeper emotional connect, bringing out something that is just an idea in your mind and moving it into your heart. A widely used coaching tool called '7 levels deep' can help determine what really drives you to accomplish anything in life. The idea is to ask 7 consecutive questions of 'why', with each answer naturally leading to the next question. You can apply this process to better understand your relationship outcomes.

Take some time out in your journal to complete this exercise. First identify what it is you want. Taking the example here of money, it could be, 'I want more money.' Then ask yourself why is having more money important to you? Next build on the last answer; for example if the answer was to be financially free, ask 'Why is being financially free important to me?' Keep asking yourself this question of why until you get to the seventh answer. When you keep asking that question, it will lead you to connect to your heart and soul and motivate you towards success in that area.

To deepen the process, you can then ask yourself how it makes you feel when you think about achieving that outcome. Focus all of your energy on that feeling. When you have achieved what you want, remember to set a new outcome you'd like to achieve. This keeps you on a path of growth, which helps you to feel fulfilled. Have you noticed that when you achieve something you want to share it with others? You do this as it leads to feeling more fulfilment.

**Think of a time you manifested what you wanted in the past. What did you do to achieve it?**

Appreciating what you already have also helps you attract more of it into your life. In summary, get focused and clear on what you want, ask why it is important to you, keep thinking about it and take 'inspiraction'! To help reach your goal, continuously work towards to it, learn from others who have already achieved it, review your progress and change your approach if necessary, until you get to the desired outcome.

## The garden of love

*It is the thoughts we water each day that become the garden we live in.*

Let's take the analogy of a garden in association with love and relationships. For the garden to thrive and produce the fruits and harvest you desire through the many changing seasons of nature, you need to become aware and notice where to pay attention to help it flourish and grow. Here I am also referring to the garden of your mind and heart. Think about what you want in your relationship. What are you creating either for yourself or together and where is your focus? What are you feeding your mind, body and spirit? Are there weeds that need attention? If so, you need to become aware of them; clear them from the roots and start to plant new seeds. What is the condition of the soil? Does it need treatment or fertiliser? What do you want to grow? What is your desired outcome?

Just as we protect our garden by ensuring we clear, nurture and plant only what we require, we need to protect ourselves from the thoughts, actions and conditions that might cause damage to ourselves and others. Without the right amount of love, care and attention, there is little or no growth. Similarly, we become what we focus upon and feed ourselves with. Our relationships need the same level of attention, acceptance and appreciation to flourish.

> ### Be the gardener of your life
>
> *My father-in-law would come around and plant vegetables, spinach, tomatoes and herbs in our garden. Whilst, I was grateful for his efforts, I thought to myself, how will we have the time to take care of the garden? Although we tried hard to maintain it, the vegetables got out of control. Slugs and weeds started appearing and we couldn't keep up with the overgrowth or eat the produce fast enough. On reflection, the more I criticised the situation, the more it got out of control. It was a metaphor for what was going on in my life. I felt overwhelmed with challenges and not having enough quality time to spend with myself or my partner.*
>
> *In comparison, a friend of mine who loves gardening and planting vegetables takes the time out to talk to her plants in an encouraging way and tends to them daily with a lot of love and appreciation. Every year she enjoys the most delicious vegetables with little effort and ease.*

These situations led me to become more aware of my thoughts and the future they were creating. Be careful of what thoughts you are planting in your mind. Are you creating weeds, flowers or fruits? Be the gardener of your life and take control of what you want from your relationships. When you pay careful attention to your thoughts with intention, tend to the limiting beliefs and stories, focus all your attention and energy towards what you want and how you want to feel, you become much happier. Give yourself time, patience, love and care to focus on what matters most so that you can enjoy your relationships and life. **How do you choose to create your garden of love?**

### Are you a gardener or a flower in your relationship?

Let's take the analogy that it needs both a gardener and a flower, a giver and taker, for a relationship to work. The gardener is the caretaker and nurtures the flower with love, whilst the flower needs that love, appreciation and attention in order to flourish. In the past, there were more women who were gardeners. However, today there are more men who are the gardeners and taking care of the flowers. There needs to be a healthy balance and understanding of each other's roles and needs to make the relationship work. Often some of the best relationships have dual roles and put in equal effort as gardeners and take turns to be flowers.

## Step 2 is the Acceptance Bridge

*'Acceptance creates the soil in which the flower of love blooms.'*
*– Brahma Kumaris*

Once you've become aware of your current reality or truth, you can work towards accepting where you are, then decide what outcome you want to move towards. Improve what you can change and accept what you can't. It sounds simple, yet many clients have difficulty accepting themselves or others.

---

**Exercise: Awareness of acceptance**

**Now ask yourself:**

1.  *What does acceptance mean to you?*

2.  *Why should you have acceptance?*

3.  *What are the consequences of not accepting?*

---

### *Learning to accept*

*I'd like to share a story of a woman who didn't accept her partner and judged him for his addiction to alcohol. It resulted in a breakdown of communication as she was unable to connect with him. She became resentful, defensive and blamed him because she couldn't accept the situation. She would vent her frustration displaying her anger at her partner, which led to physical abuse and violence. Nothing got resolved; things only got worse. He avoided her completely and drank more. She became more anxious, leading to physical health issues and stress at work. She came to me to change her partner, his behaviours and habits. After applying the Breakthrough Bridge to Love Method on herself, she finally came to terms with accepting herself and released all the stored anger, hurt and sadness in a safe way. This helped to heal her body, mind and spirit and come to forgiveness with the situation. She felt more compassion for herself and accepted what was driving her partner's behaviour.*

**Acceptance process:**

**If you are currently in a relationship, write down the answers to the following questions:**

1. *What are the things that bother me about my partner?*

2. *What can I change?*

3. *What can I never change?*

4. *Write I know I can't change this ..................................................(insert whatever it is here).*

5. *What can I accept?*

   *Learn to accept it!*

**If you are single, write down the answers to these questions:**

1. What bothers me about myself or others in relationships?

2. What do I accept about myself or others in relationships?

3. What don't I accept about myself?

4. What can I never accept?

5. What can I change about myself?

6. What can I do to start accepting myself?

## Step 3 is the Action Bridge

> *'If you always do what you've always done, you'll always get what you've always got.'* – Henry Ford

**It's that simple!** Without taking any action there is no possibility of change. You can't expect to sit there and wait for things to just fall into your lap or do nothing in the hope that things will change all by themselves or depend on someone else to sort it out for you. *For things to change, you have to change, so start doing something different today, no matter how small.*

If you want to move forward and transform your relationships, an absolute must is to take action! **What do you need to start to do differently today to create the results that you want?** You are now on your way to planting the right thoughts to take you on a journey of growth.

Every challenge gives you the opportunity to re-assess yourself and where you are heading. There is nothing you can do to change your past; it's already happened. No amount of thinking and analysing it is going to change it. You can however *choose to learn from the past and move forward with your life.*

Even in this present moment, all you can do is start to accept and from this place create your future by progressing slightly forward. I'm not suggesting you go into your future and start living there either, as that is where the anxiety can build and it can create a bigger gap, especially if you compare it to where you are currently.

**If you are depressed, you are living in the past. If you are living in the future, you are anxious. Learn to accept and live in the present moment.**

There are many lessons to learn along the way. The past is where you learned the lesson and the present moment is where you apply the lesson to create the future. *The present is all there is. It's where your dreams become a possibility. It's a precious gift.*

## Results vs. excuses?

Do you want results in your life or are you creating excuses? People come up with so many excuses sometimes that it's unbelievable! It's done either as a means of self-sabotage or procrastination. For example:

'I just don't have the time or money or energy right now.'

'I'm ok where I am.'

'He/she/they need to change.'

'The right person will just appear into my life magically without me having to do anything!'

'This feels like too much hard work.'

'I don't think I'll be able to do it!'

'I don't think this will work for me.'

'I'll think about it and maybe try tomorrow.'

The list of excuses just goes on and on. Regardless of the excuse used, if you continue to use it, it will lead you to a result you don't want. Just take a look at your current life and the results; this is a good indication of the truth. You are the creator of everything you have or are going through in your life.

> 'It's in the moments of our decisions where our destiny is shaped.'
> – Tony Robbins

If you want to take charge of your life and the **results** that you get, then there are **no excuses**; only the **decisions, choices** and **actions** that you take. Focus on the possibilities.

**Exercise: Let's get into the action**

1. *Think of 3 reasons that stop you from taking action, even when you know that by taking this action it will change your life.*

2. *What are the consequences of you not taking action?*

3. *What or who inspires you to take action?*

4. *Why do you want to do this, or why is it important to you?*

5. *Think of a time in your life when you took action and made a change. What did you do and what was the result? It could be as simple as starting to eat healthier or exercising which led to increased energy levels and becoming fitter.*

6. *What is one small step you can take today to progress in an area of your relationship, either with yourself or another?*

7. *When are you committed to start?*

Sometimes we spend so long figuring out how things will happen that we forget about why we are doing them in the first place. *If your why is big enough, you will find a way and the universe will conspire to make the how happen for you.*

### Buffet time

*Have you ever been for a buffet meal? There are so many different foods to choose from that you don't even know where to start. Do you get stuck on the starters and fill yourself up so that you never reach the mains or dessert? Or do you start with the mains or rush straight for dessert? Are you someone who digs in and samples a little of everything and eats too quickly so that it becomes hard to digest anything?* **Notice how you do anything is probably how you do everything in your life.** *If you are not disciplined in one area of your life, the chances are it will* *affect other areas of your life. Building upon the buffet analogy, just keep it simple. Pick one area you want to work on. Complete that first, enjoy the learnings and digest it fully before deciding to move onto the next area. Don't forget to pause and celebrate your progress in between before rushing from one thing to another, as it will help you focus on the results you want to create in your life.*

Remember that motion creates emotion. Start to move and consciously engage with life. It's so much easier to remain the same until you either get a wake-up call or things get so bad that you have no choice but to move. Take those baby steps towards learning, growing and becoming the best version of yourself!

> *'The secret to change is to focus all of your energy, not on fighting the old, but on building the new.' – Socrates*

It is a continuous journey of self-discovery depending on the lessons you came here to learn this lifetime. **Are you ready to face the truth and have the courage to let go of your limitations, breakthrough your barriers and bridge the love gap?**

It doesn't matter how many times you have felt hurt in the past or had your heart broken, or how desperate you have been to make your relationships work... with the right guidance, cutting edge tools and the **Bridge to Love Method,** you can breakthrough and heal your life on all levels and connect with the **true you.**

# Chapter 4

# Mindset Bridge

*'You cannot fix a problem with the same level of thinking that created it.' – Albert Einstein*

In this chapter, you will learn some powerful tools to **master your mindset and thoughts** so that you feel more focused, **gain clarity** to make **better decisions** and have **peace of mind** in your relationships.

## Master your mindset

Life doesn't happen to you. It happens for you! How you see the world, other people and yourself is just your perception. *Your past conditioning influences how you see things in the present.* Therefore, as Dr. Wayne Dyer says, **'If you change the way you look at things, the things you look at change.'** By changing your perception, the things you experience around you will change.

Your **mental body** or mindset is about having **clarity of vision** around your **mission;** it's knowing what you want. This gives you the ability to navigate through life and **make decisions to move forward.** The secret lies in understanding how to connect with your brain, master and train your mindset and shift your thinking and physiology to create the desired results.

## Training your mindset

When we worry or tell ourselves that we are scared, it affects our physiology and can prevent us from taking action. Worrying about something that happened in the past or hasn't even taken place yet causes anxiety and fear. Your brain doesn't know the difference between the energy of fear and excitement as it recognises it as the same emotion. It's like being on a rollercoaster; you can find it hard to distinguish between the excitement and the fear. Excitement is like fear wearing a smile.

**There are no good or bad relationships. The only thing that matters is you** and what your current mindset and quality of thoughts are like. You literally attract into your life what you think about and create your own reality.

What I am referring to here is the mindset, not the brain. The brain is an organ that controls the functioning of the nervous system, whilst the **mindset enables a person to become aware of the world through their perceptions and thoughts.**

Your thoughts and words impact the way you see the world. When you send these out, they carry a certain energetic vibration. This vibration colours the lens with which you view the world. There are different stages of development as you learn to tap into your own personal vibration, whether that is through meditation, breathing, singing, yoga, or dancing. You begin to trust yourself and listen inwardly. There is a small voice within, your personal consciousness. You need to control your thought processes to quieten this voice and train the mind to find stillness.

> **What if you could be an observer of your thoughts to create happy loving thoughts?**

Through regular practice, you can relax the mind and come into 'the zone', becoming an observer of your thoughts. This is where you connect with spirit, your intuition and your heart speak.

**Exercise: Achieving outcomes**

Now take some time to reflect in you journal. Think for a moment of something you have already achieved in your life or relationship and answer the following questions:

1. What were the thoughts that led you there?

2. How did you feel and what actions did you take?

3. What did you specifically do to create the outcome?

## Focusing your thoughts

As it all starts with your thoughts, it's important to focus on the quality of your thinking. According to Abraham-Hicks, **17 seconds of pure thought is the ignition point of manifesting**. If you hold a thought for 17 seconds, you set in motion that manifestation. The longer you can focus and hold these pure thoughts, say building **up to 70 seconds,** the more these thoughts will affect you. The highest vibration of thought always wins. Your mind is more powerful than you can ever imagine. It stores and processes every thought, emotion, and event you ever had at a subconscious level, which in turn affects your perception and creates your reality. Thoughts start to become things.

Did you know that the average person has around 70,000 thoughts a day! That's a great number of thoughts and if most of them are repetitive or unproductive then it's time to become aware and re-programme them. Most of these thoughts end up becoming the stories we tell ourselves in our minds.

Every thought you think, word you speak, action you take, plays a part in your relationships. They create a ripple effect. Now take a moment to reflect in your journal and respond to the following:

- What are the consistent stressful thoughts you think about and how do they affect your day?

- What are the words you may have spoken today and the thoughts that have been running through your mind?

- Assess what type of life you are creating through your thoughts and words.

## What's your story?

*'The nature of the thinking mind is fear, doubt and judgment – a stream of imagined words, sounds and pictures passing through consciousness. The only meaning it has is the story, the meaning we invest in it. It is not real.' – Brandon Bays*

Everyone has a story they tell themselves. The quality of your story is dependent on how you think and feel about yourself, your beliefs, perceptions, values and the meaning you give to it. Some people choose to end their stories in pain, reliving them over and over again. This may also involve blaming others and becoming a victim of their circumstances. Others may become conscious and learn valuable lessons from pain, which helps them to shift their mindset, grow and turn their stories into pleasure.

Now take a moment to reflect upon the stories you are creating. Are you pursuing pain or pleasure? **What if you could create stories filled with love and joy?** All of us have different stories. We are all unique and experience similar challenges and pain depending upon what we choose to think. Some people will go through life with struggle and hardship to change, whilst others are quick to change when they are not getting the desired results. As Tony Robbins says, **'It's time to divorce your story and marry the truth!'**

### Who are you outside of your story?

I had a client who kept repeating her relationship breakup story of the past so well that she was unable to let it go, causing her much pain and suffering. She was so focused on the past and what her partner had done that it became a distraction to her attracting a future relationship. When she came to see me, I asked her how this story was serving her now. She realised that it was not; it was keeping her from meeting her dream partner. We worked through her negative thought patterns, feelings, and behaviours that were keeping the old story in place. She wrote a new, powerful story from a place of awareness and intention to connect to the best version of herself. She became more focused, started dating and attracting love into her life.

**Exercise: The stories you tell yourself**

**Take a moment to reflect on the following in your journal, using the Triple 'A' Bridge Formula.**

**Awareness:**

Think for a moment about all the stories you tell yourself about yourself and your relationships. Consider who else may have contributed to these stories. Become mindful of the meaning you are giving your stories. You are only human and have both negative and positive thoughts. You need both to be balanced. The key is to practice and come into awareness.

Challenge yourself to question your stories and the thoughts you are thinking, so that you can start to become aware and work towards creating the results you want in your life.

**Acceptance:**

Start accepting whatever is coming up from a place of compassion, even if it is a story that makes you feel uncomfortable. Just stop and become aware. Accept whatever you are thinking with no judgement.

**Action:**

Now you can start to replace your unhelpful or destructive thoughts with better ones.

When you notice yourself thinking something negative about someone or being self-critical or judgemental, repeat the word 'cancel' to yourself. This sends a message to your brain to shift focus. Then repeat the statement with a better thought. This way you are retraining your subconscious mind and creating a new conscious mental muscle and way of being. **If you can master your thoughts, you can master your life to achieve what you want.** You just need to give the mind a job to do. Instead of letting it control you, guide it with clear instructions and quality questions so you feel more in control.

Here are some examples in relationships of how this plays out.

## Why can't they change?

*'Everything that irritates us about others can lead us to an understanding of ourselves.' – Carl Jung*

Many clients complain and say that their partners are lazy. They either don't listen to them or feel they should be doing more. They want their partner to change and behave in a certain way around them. However, people should not be defined by their behaviours. We often get irritated and judge people based on their attitudes and behaviour, whether it is their anger, avoidance, disrespect, addictions or betrayal, etc. Know that there is a great deal of pain beneath for that person and an avoidance of dealing with their issues that leads them to act out in a certain way. Usually their behaviour is never about you, although it may feel like it at the time. It says more about them as a person. They realise this when they become aware of the consequences of their action, which may bring about change. Remember, you can only work to change yourself and not another person.

> ### Shifting focus
>
> A housewife came to see me as her husband had a habit of getting angry for no apparent reason. She did her best to stay positive around him, although his anger affected her moods and dimmed

her light. She felt anxious and shut down. During our sessions together, she realised that the problem was not his anger (i.e. the behaviour displayed). She discovered through his eyes that he felt unworthy and uncertain, telling himself that he disliked his job and had failed in his career. These negative thoughts led to him projecting his anger outward. It was his coping mechanism to feel heard and seen and made him feel significant.

Through coaching, she shifted her focus to what would give her happiness. She realised she could not fix him. She started valuing herself by focusing on what she loved doing, whilst accepting and encouraging him with his career. Within a short time, he felt inspired to change careers and started doing what he loved. He became more compassionate and loving towards her, his communication improved and the anger towards her stopped. There was more love and connection between them.

Sometimes, it just takes one person in the relationship to come into awareness of their situation. With a little shift in thinking and focus, everything changes and starts to fall into place.

*"If I want to be loved as I am, I have to be willing to love others as they are" – Louise Hay*

Humans naturally look at how to fix things in a relationship, instead of seeing things as they are, or accepting themselves or the other person as they are. Rather than looking to fix someone, focus on what you can change within; do things that make you happy, so you become a better version of yourself every day. To enhance your relationships, ask yourself **how can I be a better person?** When you want more love and happiness, you need to give that to others who will reciprocate it. Then watch as you become happier.

# Love beyond belief – bridging beliefs

*Whether you believe you can do something or not is all up to you.*

Your beliefs affect everything you choose to do, and create your experience of the world. **A belief is a habit of thought**. We are born into a particular belief system, yet our beliefs are always a choice.

We come into the world full of infinite love, light, pure awareness and boundless energy. As we grow up, we may learn to become fearful and develop disempowering beliefs from experiences, the environment and the people that surround us. This, in turn, affects our confidence, happiness, wellbeing and can dim our light.

Your outer circumstances reflect what is going on within your inner world and creates a map of beliefs and perceptions you hold about yourself and others. Through the study of NLP and human development stages, I learned about behavioural patterning. This outlines that when we are born up until the age of 7 is the time where we experience the energy of care, from age 7 till 14 years we start modelling others and from ages 14 through 21 years is where we respond to our peers and are influenced by others; this is called the social period. From 21 years onwards, we live out experiences from all the information we have received both consciously and subconsciously and become coded, just like a computer programme.

## Surrounding yourself with the right people

It's essential to start to become more conscious of the people you interact with on a daily basis. Surround yourself with people who will love and support you for who you are, who encourage your dreams, who value your vision and want you to flourish and grow. Choose to spend time with people in your peer group who have a similar mindset and qualities that you admire, who inspire you to co-create a vision together. Did you know that the 5 people you spend the most time with impacts your belief system and the results in your life? So, choose wisely! It's also important not to judge but to love the people who are currently in your life, especially family members.

Now take a moment to reflect and answer these questions in your journal:

1. Who do you spend the most time with?

2. Who do you look up to in your life?

3. Do they embody the qualities you want to acquire?

For those of you who are parents, it is critical to be even more mindful of your thoughts, behaviours and actions. This in turn programmes your child's internal coding as they start to learn about life and forms an imprint as they grow into adults.

Beliefs are so powerful as initially other people tell us something and then we tell ourselves the same information as if it is our truth. One belief that a client shared with me was that it 'runs in the family', assuming that is was just the way things were. They were only able to change this belief when they came into awareness of it. Beliefs can be passed down from generation to generation, so it's even more important to become aware of these patterns of thought and where they are leading you. If these beliefs are limiting, they can hold you back from living your full expression and loving fully. Telling yourself things like 'I'm not good enough', 'I can't do this', 'life is a struggle', etc. can lead to procrastination and dissatisfaction. Feeling 'not good enough' is a universal subconscious belief that shows up for many. It can lead to sabotage in relationships or can result in you pushing yourself to achieving more just to prove your worth to others.

The beliefs you have about yourself can either empower or disempower you from taking inspiration. Truly believing in yourself and communicating that you are loveable, that anything is possible, and things are always working out for you, will lift your spirits and help you become more resourceful.

### Accessing your body's wisdom

Just thinking positively and repeating positive affirmations alone is not enough. You need to have a strong belief. Having tested this theory out by observing the physiology of a person, and matching it to their words and energy levels, was a good indicator that it wasn't sustainable. For example, have you noticed a time where you might not have been feeling too great and no matter how much you told yourself you were feeling great, it just didn't work? To get the optimum results, it is best to access your body's wisdom by listening and tuning into the truth of what you are feeling in that moment. The body has an intellect of its own. This will guide you to the root cause of any issue and the underlying core belief. The next step is to address and clear out whatever may be stopping you from feeling good. From this space you will feel more aligned and be able to create new empowering beliefs and positive affirmations, which will support you to bridging the love gap and live an inspiractional life.

Now we will work towards getting your beliefs into harmony.

**The first step is to uncover your unconscious beliefs and identify them.**

**Take some time to reflect in your journal on how your life conditioning, beliefs and the stories you tell yourself have helped or hindered you. Start to become an observer of them. What is your default programming?**

- Where did you learn these beliefs?

- What is your truth?

- How do these beliefs/stories and programming affect your current reality and future?

Remember your thoughts are powerful and become things. It's time to breakthrough these beliefs and create a new way of being to connect to the truth of who you are and what is important to you. When you do this, you start to feel aligned and much more becomes possible for you.

The client story below illustrates the power of beliefs and how you get what you focus on.

### What you believe is what you see

A client of mine who was single had a belief that happy marriages don't exist, therefore she chose not to get married. I asked her how she knew this to be true. She replied that she didn't know of or hasn't seen any happily married couples around her. She also shared that her parents had a bad relationship. I asked her to reflect and notice what she was looking for – happy or unhappy married couples? She became quiet. I watched as something clicked for her. I noticed how her use of language and watching her parent's relationship had led her to create this belief, which had formed the basis of her experience of the world. She had therefore kept herself closed off from marriage and chose to stay single. I explained how this reaffirms the pattern by helping the brain stack up evidence and look for ways to support our belief system.

We worked on clearing the energy around the old belief and creating a new empowering belief to 'see happy couples everywhere'. She started to reinforce this through daily practice. Soon enough, she began to see evidence and stories of happily married couples in various ways, from reading about celebrity stories, or seeing couples having fun together out in shopping malls and restaurants. It was a remarkable shift to see how her new focus and choice of thoughts led her to think and feel differently. She felt much happier within and considered attracting a relationship and marriage.

Witness your beliefs without judgment. What experience from your past is causing you to experience this now? Find evidence to the contrary. Actively look for the opposite belief. Where it is true, the more you see it, the more believe it.

---

### Exercise: Beliefs to attract a partner

If you have a desire to attract a life partner, take some time to reflect and write the answers to these questions in your journal:

- Who do you want to be as a partner?

- What are you bringing to the relationship?

- What new beliefs do you need to create so that you can attract your life partner?

**Write them all down and notice how it makes you feel.**

**Here are some examples of empowering beliefs:**

- My ideal partner is available and I can attract them with ease

- Good men/women exist

- I am worthy of love and a relationship

- It is safe for me to feel free and express myself with my life partner

- I am willing to accept that I'm smart enough, loveable and have what it takes within and my partner fully supports me

---

## Beliefs about money

Another core area that is linked to relationships is money. Let's take a look at how you can align your beliefs in this area.

A client had set up a belief that to be successful with a partner, she would need a certain amount of money and to work long hours to match up to that belief. In truth, conscious men value support, love and connection from women.

Do you think you need to earn a certain amount of money before you are in love? How can you feel like an equal with your partner?

Money disagreements or a lack of open and constructive conversations about money is one of the major causes of conflict in relationships. It is best to be clear and upfront about financial issues, to set ground rules and take responsibility for your finances. Practicing honesty and agreeing how money should be spent will help to resolve conflict and avoid resentment later.

Using powerful beliefs aided with visualisation can assist you to manifest more money and abundance into your life. You may have even heard about the actor and comedian Jim Carey, who wrote himself a cheque for $10 million and dated it ten years into the future. He kept it in his wallet and looked at it daily. Ten years later he was cast in the movie 'Dumb and Dumber' and rewarded exactly $10 million. This was only possible as he had a clear image of exactly what he wanted in his life and had a strong belief that it would happen. My point here is that you can attract whatever you want into your life just by thinking, feeling and hearing it. Writing things down and then getting into a dream state to visualise achieving it will accelerate your ability to manifest your dreams.

Let's now take a look at how you can bridge your beliefs in relationships.

---

**Exercise: Bridging beliefs**

**What are some of the beliefs that you grew up with around relationships, men or women?**

To uncover the beliefs that may be keeping you stuck, the following exercise can assist in tapping into your subconscious mind and transforming these beliefs into conscious thoughts so you can make a shift. Once anything comes into your conscious awareness it is much easier to work with it. Give yourself plenty of time and space to do this powerful exercise. If you begin to notice whilst writing that you become emotional, just allow these emotions to flow through. They are coming up to be cleared and healed. If a story arises, do not get attached. Just stay with the emotion.

---

In your journal write each of the following statements at the top of each page and make a note of whatever comes into your mind. Just allow the words to flow. Keep writing until you feel it's complete.

Men are...

Women are ...

Love is ...

Relationships are...

I'm lonely because...

**Read out loud what you have written and consider how these thoughts compare to your life right now. Circle any repetitive thoughts.**

**Now ask yourself:**

What do you believe about your situation?

How do your beliefs reflect your current situation?

**What insights did you gain after completing this exercise?**

To breakthrough these negative thought patterns it is necessary to do some energetic clearing. Just flipping your beliefs from disempowering into empowering ones is not enough.

---

**I am who I am. It is safe to be me.**

I worked with a client who told me that although she worked very hard, others felt disappointed with her work. It was causing her to make mistakes and experience an overwhelming frustration. When I asked her to tune into her body and consider how it made her feel, she uncovered a lot of shame in her solar plexus area. I guided her to stay with her body and the emotions that surfaced. She felt the frustration and was then able to access the various emotional layers underneath. The root cause of this frustration was her parents consistently telling her she was not good enough as a child. I could see how this limiting belief was linked to her working hard and pushing herself to achieve more and feel appreciated.

As she released these negative emotions, her physiology changed, and she became much calmer and more present. At the end of the session, she made a choice to take some time out for herself. This was only possible as she felt more aligned to her new empowering beliefs of feeling loved and safe to be herself. It made a huge difference to her as she became more relaxed, was able to focus and produce high quality work in less time.

**Your past does not equal your future.**

You are not ultimately limited by your past. However, until you become aware of your programming and conditioning, you will continue to live out the patterns that were created from the past. Your memories take you back into the past, whilst your dreams will move you forward. It's therefore advisable not to spend ages dwelling in the past and instead work to clear and create happy memories. You have the ability to consciously observe your belief systems and choose a new way of being in a relationship. **Awareness is the bridge to transformation and loving beyond belief.** You can create a new future for yourself if you choose to.

In what ways could your past programming be affecting you?

**What new empowering beliefs would you like to create for yourself?**

## How can I break free to love?

Just to be clear I am not suggesting for you to break free and come out of a relationship if you are in one. It's exactly the opposite. It's about breaking free of your inner limitations and negative thought forms and patterns so that you can learn to accept and love all of yourself.

You can then bring those qualities into your relationship and create the life you truly desire from a place of unconditional love and being free to express yourself. That's the real breakthrough!

## 1. Catch yourself

When you feel your buttons are being pushed by something or someone, and have those negative feelings of frustration or anger, it may cause you to get defensive and do or say something that you may later regret. Our words and actions are so powerful and unfortunately, once we let them out, we can't take them back.

Take a moment to reflect in your journal and answer the following:

- What are some of the words that others use that may trigger you?

- What are the words that you use that may trigger others?

This whole process, from the time you are triggered to how you respond, is a gap. The smaller the gap in this process, the more destructive you could become if you let your thinking mind take control.

To break free, you need to begin the practice of catching yourself to widen this gap. Bring conscious awareness to what is happening in your thought process and change the response, so you can make better choices and create more harmony in your relationships. It also helps to remember that the people or situations who push your buttons are just messengers who help heal parts of your being.

## 2. Challenge your thoughts

One process, taken from The Work of Byron Katie, enables people to become aware of the quality of their thinking. They challenge their thoughts by applying these four questions:

1. Is it true?

2. Can you absolutely know that it's true?

3. How do you react, what happens, when you believe that thought?

4. Who would you be without that thought?

---

### Who would you be without your thoughts?

I had a client who kept having a repetitive thought that her partner didn't love or care about her. She came to this conclusion after he had not responded to her in the way she expected. This made her feel unloved. He would respond with the silent treatment causing her to feel upset and resulted in a distance in their communication. When she self-enquired through this process, she came to realise all the ways in which she had been uncaring. She started to notice the things that her partner did for her, which she hadn't even acknowledged before. It was proof that he cared. This made her feel loved and she started appreciating her partner more. When I asked her who she would be without those thoughts, she felt fully free at that moment and created a new thought, which was 'I love and care for my partner unconditionally and he loves and cares for me.'

---

Some other questions to ask yourself are:

- Does this thought bring me joy?

- Does this thought move me closer or pull me away from love?

If it doesn't then let it go!

### 3. Journaling

Writing is an excellent way to capture your thoughts, become reflective and start questioning them. It's also a way to externalise and express your feelings and can help you gain awareness, clarity and feel lighter. It reinforces daily learning too. I would encourage you to make this a daily practice, so that you discover it's benefits.

### 4. Analyse your thought patterns

Set a daily timer, depending on what may be convenient for you. This may be every hour if you are a compulsive thinker. This will enable you to stop and ask yourself what you are thinking at that moment. What are your persistent thoughts? What do you think about when you are working, cooking, cleaning or taking a shower?

## Conscious cleansing

I caught myself, having a disagreement with someone in my mind, whilst I was taking a shower. The same thoughts were going around in my mind and I kept recalling the event and analysing what was said and not said. I started to become consciously aware of my thoughts in that moment by pausing and became present to them. I took a few deep breaths which helped me to let go and feel calmer. I imagined my negative thoughts as dark colours that were being washed away with the water and started visualising white light entering into my body. I was having a conscious cleanse of my thoughts and it felt wonderfully relaxing.

Reflecting back on my life, I realise that I was given every experience, challenge, and person to purposely push my buttons, helping me break free. They were my most valuable messengers who helped me to move through the negative patterns and learn some very powerful lessons to discover the truth of who I was becoming, loving myself and living my life purpose.

Learning to detach in an unconditional way has been a journey of commitment, focus, and action, enabling me to feel much more connected and at peace with myself. Although some of the memories are still there, my response to the events, challenges, and people have changed and the negative patterns have lost their charge. I am more able to deal with situations from a place of understanding and compassion.

### Daily Practice: Flip the script

When a negative thought enters your mind, think up three positive ones. Reach for better thoughts and train yourself to flip the script each time. With practice you will become much more aware and focused on what you want.

## Courage

**Courage is what it takes to stand up and speak. Courage is also what it takes to sit down and listen.**

Quite often we may not follow through on something due to either our own voice in our head or listening to the opinions of others that prevents us from doing something. They create fear.

Where there is fear there is also courage. Fear is natural. It comes from our mind, which is trying to protect us and keep us safe. We need to bypass that fear and have the courage to take action on the great ideas we have every day. It takes courage to take responsibility and face up to the truth, to confront your fears head-on and be willing to turn inwards to gain clarity and break free.

---

### Exercise: Courage

In what ways have you tapped into courage to change something that wasn't working in your life?

Think of a time in your life when you faced a challenging situation.

- What did you specifically do to overcome it?

- How did that make you feel?

- What was the outcome?

---

Let's now focus on looking at problems as challenges that we can overcome. We just need to find solutions, so we can make a difference to ourselves, others and the world. **Energy flows where attention goes and what we focus on expands! Where are you choosing to focus your attention now?**

# Codes to mastering love and empowering relationships

## What are relationship codes?

Your codes around relationships are how you have been programmed through past conditioning and the experiences of who you currently believe you are. Our codes can either empower or disempower the quality of our relationships.

---

**Exercise: Creating empowering codes**

**Write down the 3 things you believe to be true about yourself and your relationships.**

Now assess your answers. If you think these beliefs no longer serve you, you can create new empowering codes.

Having powerful codes can keep you on track when things get tough in your relationship. These are things you absolutely must know to be true. You can create codes that resonate for you in your personal situation or use the examples below to help you remember what is important to you in your relationship.

I would suggest that you keep them somewhere where you can see them daily, for example in the bedroom or bathroom. This helps to make them conscious habits that are wired into your brain.

---

## Love and empowering relationship codes

1. *Quality time and space enables me to understand myself and my partner, allowing us to support one another better.*

2. *Relationships act as mirrors and enhance my personal growth.*

3. *This relationship is more important than being right.*

4. *I am not my behaviour; I am pure love.*

5. *The key to love is compassion for self and others.*

6.   *People matter more than things.*

7.   *This relationship is teaching me how to love myself.*

8.   *It's okay to wait for the right relationship instead of being in the wrong relationship.*

"

**What are your new empowering love and relationship codes?**

"

# Chapter 5

# Heart Bridge

———— ✧ ————

*'Go deep inside and you will be surprised that hate, anger and jealousy all exist on the periphery. In the innermost centre of your being, there is only love.' – Osho*

In this chapter, you will learn how to **master your emotions and connect with the heart of who you truly are** so that you can **powerfully express** yourself and come into **alignment.**

Learning how to **connect with your heart, feelings** and **intuition,** so connecting to your emotional body, helps you become more **resilient** and have more **care** and **compassion** for yourself and others. Mastering your emotions and bridging your heart helps you heal, see things for what they are and feel more balanced so that you can move forward. Your emotions can provide a wonderful guidance system for you, if only you pay attention to the meaning you give them. Mastering your emotions is the key to tapping into the endless flow of love that is always there and provides a deeper connection to your soul.

People who are more in touch with their emotional energy are open to giving love, much happier, more creative and able to make the right decisions to help them through life.

## Emotional mastery

*The inner ocean of emotion is always in motion*

All emotions whether they are joy, fear or sadness, etc. are just energies that are vibrating in the body at different frequencies. In fact, as Rumi said, '**Love is not an emotion. It is your very existence.**' Think of someone you love. Notice how the feelings in your body may be light and make you feel good. On the other hand, if you were to think of someone you dislike, it may feel heavier and not so good.

Emotions are energy in motion. All energy is frequency and carries information. Based on our thoughts and feelings, we are always sending and receiving information. Our everyday life is dictated by our emotions. There is never nothing happening. Fully feeling a range of emotions creates a living, breathing experience and makes life matter. It also creates connection. Emotions enrich us and are part of life. They are the awareness that connects you with your inner wisdom.

We can experience two sides to emotions. We may go through many stressful situations in everyday life, whether it is our work, finances or relationships which can affect our health. Negative emotions caused by these situations can become painful and difficult to deal with, especially if you do not address them or you are experiencing trauma.

People often look to distract themselves by going out to have fun, socialise or drink to move away from dealing with their emotions. You may have experienced these short-term releases that provide enjoyment in the moment. It's okay to take a break if you are not feeling up to it, yet many go through life stuck on an emotional loop, repeating negative patterns where thoughts and beliefs produce unhelpful feelings, that further intensify if they do not do the inner work. This can result in attracting the same relationships or challenges over and over in your life. Relying on external resources alone may address the effects but not the cause of the issue.

### From heartbreak to joy

I worked with a client who went through a breakup and kept herself busy with work to keep her mind off things, yet all the while she felt sad and heartbroken and kept ruminating over what went wrong in the relationship. I could see that by her dwelling on these unproductive thoughts she was stuck in a repetitive loop, making her feel sad and not able to focus on anything else. Instead of going into the story of her breakup, I guided her to focus on her heart, open up and fully feel her emotions. After releasing them she was able to gain fresh insights about herself and the relationship. This enabled her to create empowering thought patterns leading to feelings of joy. She began to re-engage with life, taking the needed time out to care for her emotional health. She is now in a new relationship and is living with her partner.

Most importantly, you have the ability to choose your emotional state in any given moment and not be a victim of life. There are no good or bad emotions. Some emotions add renewal and quality to our lives, whilst others deplete us and prevent us from having pleasure. Did you know that every time you make an emotional shift from anger to calm, love to anxiety, etc., biochemical changes take place inside you and affect your body for hours? Depleting emotions release stress hormones such as cortisol and adrenalin, affecting health, whilst experiencing renewing emotions, produces regenerative hormones such as oxytocin (love), helping you to recharge and increase your resilience.

Let's take a look at some common challenging emotions that are experienced in relationships when things get tough, which can cause stress, pressure, disappointment, etc. and examine what can be done to manage them.

**Fear** – is only natural and occurs when there is a need to change something. For example, the need to prepare for something that is going to happen, such as speaking in front of a group or having a difficult conversation.

**Anger** – is where you have a rule that has been violated or you have violated your own rules. Anger can be powerful when expressed in the right way, or destructive if not controlled. Keep it in balance.

**Sadness** – is an emotional pain associated with the loss of a loved one or occurs after a breakup. It can be connected to an external event or person. There is great intelligence in sadness as it means your heart is open to healing. Sadness allows us to be empathetic and hold ourselves in love. Giving yourself the necessary time out to process through it will help you to move forward.

**Hurt** – occurs when an expectation you have is not being met or you take things personally. Focus on what you do want now, not on why you feel hurt. Acknowledge it and work towards changing the way you communicate with yourself and others.

**Frustration** – is when what you are doing is not working out or another person is not understanding your needs. You need to learn about yourself, be willing to change and be flexible to resolve the issue.

**Guilt** – is experienced when you have dishonoured your values or standards, or someone else's, and are living in the past. Alternatively, you may feel you have done something wrong or could have done more. Learn from it and commit you are not going to do it again.

The meaning you attach to certain experiences will affect the way you feel. For example, if you've disagreed with your partner and it feels challenging, ask yourself if you want to be right or you want to be in love? Is the relationship more important to you than the disagreement? Focus on the outcome you want.

**Which emotions do you experience on a daily basis?**

---

### Exercise: Pressure points

Imagine a pressure cooker. Once it gets to boiling point, the whistle blows and it lets off steam. With unhealthy emotions like anger or rage, if you keep them boiling up inside of you and don't release them in a healthy way, they can cause internal pressure in your system and eventually become an illness.

Take some time to reflect in your journal and answer the following:

- Where do you put unnecessary pressure on yourself? Notice how you do this. Is it internal or external pressure?

---

- Who or what pushes your buttons?

- In what ways can you release this pressure?

Consider when was the last time you gave yourself permission to just be playful and stop taking life so seriously. Take time out to relieve the pressure. List all the ways you can do this.

## Wake-up calls

Sometimes we may even get a wake-up call. It's a warning that something isn't right as we've not listened to our emotions. These can come in the form of a diagnosed illness or simply reading or watching something on the news triggers something inside us. Don't wait for the wake-up call. Pay attention now.

Emotional issues become stored inside our bodies, forming memories at a cellular level. When we feel emotions, we release biochemistry in the body. When a strong emotion comes up, we often get into motion; whether it is watching Netflix, getting on social media, calling a friend, etc., we avoid it at all costs rather than befriend it. The way to befriend your emotions is to acknowledge and welcome them. You will get to the root cause by accessing any suppressed memories that may surface when you focus within your body. This will help you to uncover what you have been repressing and see the real issues so that you understand, accept, release and come to forgiveness. Your mind and body can then come to a place of peace.

External circumstances are not the real cause of an issue. The issue was already inside you. A situation or person pushes your buttons, the fear and anger come up and we project it onto others through blame. Blame is an avoidance of meeting the pain. When things go on outside, we can look within, listening to our intuition and so feel at home in our skin.

> ### What's in your cup?
>
> Imagine you are holding a cup of coffee when someone comes along and bumps into you, making you spill your coffee everywhere. Why did you spill the coffee? You spilled the coffee because there was coffee in your cup. Had there been tea in the cup you would have spilled tea. The point is that whatever is inside the cup, is what will spill out. Therefore, when life comes along and shakes you, which will happen, whatever is inside you will come out. It's easy to fake it until you get rattled. So, we have to ask ourselves, what's in my cup? When life gets tough, what spills out? Is your cup filled with joy, peace and love? Or does anger, resent, and blame come out? You choose! Let's work towards being conscious of what we are filling our cups with. Let's start with affirming gratitude, forgiveness, kind words, love and compassion for others.

## It's safe to feel

I've worked with people who at first felt completely shut down or ashamed of their emotions. Some had even labelled themselves with depression. Gradually, after creating a safe space and building trust, they were able to welcome their emotions and connect to themselves. Depression can keep you stuck, stopping you from living to your true potential, whereas fully feeling emotions, such as anger, can help to break through depression and move you forward.

It's like turning a tap on which hasn't been opened in a long time. At first the water may drip out slowly. Then as you feel more comfortable and safe, you learn to open, soften and allow the emotions to be freely expressed and just flow. They can't hurt, only heal you.

If you think about young babies or children, when they get upset, they just express their emotions; they don't hold back. They are so present and aware. Yet as we grow older, we become afraid of the consequences of being seen as too emotional, sensitive or needy.

Most people in relationships don't really know how to deal with their emotions or support their partner emotionally. I've seen this in particular with men who are wired to wanting to fix the problem and women who are identified as being either too mothering, sensitive or liable to over-react. This can be a major cause of conflict. Instead consider the needs of the other and ask how you can best support them.

If you have ever felt stuck emotionally or didn't feel safe to express yourself, some of the reasons could be due to fear of the response and outcome i.e. rejection, abandonment or getting hurt. Some people choose to avoid feeling their emotions as that seems safer than facing any such situation.

The consequence of unresolved emotions, where you don't deal with stress and anxiety levels in your relationships, can lead to physical symptoms later. This can be severe, with serious illnesses manifesting, such as heart and lung disease and all forms of cancer. In fact, 90% of cancer is made up of lifestyle and belief system. This is backed up by studies done by the Centre for Disease Control in the US who say **85% of all illness has a root cause in emotional stress**.

My mother often repressed her emotions to keep the peace at home. She was unable to effectively let go of negative emotions in a healthy way. Over time her body manifested this as cancer in the liver.

Through love and acceptance for yourself, you can transform negative emotions into sweetness. Rather than repressing, it's about fully feeling without becoming attached. Witness, allow and then release emotions in a detached way to live a healthy life.

**How different ego personality types deal with anger**

*You cannot see your reflection in boiling water. Similarly, you cannot see the truth in a state of anger. When the waters calm, clarity comes.*

Your **ego** is your conscious mind, the part of your identity that you consider your 'self', your self-esteem or self-importance. The ego starts to develop during the first five years of a child's life. When the ego is at play, it can keep you separate from others and yourself. The reason behind most conflicts is often where there is ego present. The ego wants to be right. Through direct experience at the Journey Intensive Healing Retreats, I had powerful insights that the ego is nothing more than the core fixation patterns that shape types of the personality self and drive certain behaviours. When these unhealthy patterns play out, you identify with them as your real self. Exposing these patterns can allow you to connect to a deeper truth, have more compassion for yourself and others, and respond differently in your relationships. Our higher self wants us to be at peace and happy. **When you have a choice, to be right or to be kind, always choose kindness. Do it with everyone that crosses your path.**

Below I will share some common ego types that are connected to anger being projected or held back. Anger is usually a response to fear, coming from the ego. It relates to the way that you look at yourself.

**Controllers:** Have you noticed that people who have strong controlling tendencies usually project their anger outwards onto people and situations?

**Peacemakers** on the other hand tend to avoid conflict. Those born as a **middle child or second born** are more likely to take on this role in the family or their environments. They are good at mediating and negotiating and become passively aggressive, keeping their emotions stored inside to keep the peace and resolve arguments as they prefer things to go with the flow.

**Perfectionist** tendencies are useful and best applied when you are feeling balanced or working on something that may need careful precision, for example if you work as a surgeon, or auditor. However, when under stress, it may cause you to be too hard on yourself and not feel safe to make mistakes. Therefore, you try and over control everything and possibly project that anger outwards onto others or internally within. This anger may come up from conditioning yet is usually connected to memories from your past. Making mistakes can help you to grow and teach you valuable lessons.

**Which of these ego types resonates for you?**

**How different cultures deal with emotions**

My journey has led me to become an observer of different people, their energies and how they deal with their emotions.

In the UK, where I have lived for many years, I have noticed that some British people are quite reserved and find it hard to initially open up and share their emotions. On the other hand, they are also some of the most emotional people I know. For example, just watch the country compete in the World Cup or come together in a time of crisis.

The way we emote has much to do with our upbringing, culture and values.

---

**I'm line**

*It reminds me of one on my UK clients, Samantha, who would initially just respond 'I'm fine' when asked about anything. It felt like she had put a massive energetic barrier up which pushed people away. She was a very private person and when I connected with her she told me she felt a deep sadness, was very lonely and didn't have many friends at work or in her social circle. She started to open up to me and over time our conversations gained a real depth. We successfully worked on her becoming more comfortable with expressing her emotions. She became much more open with people, confident and happy about life.*

---

Have you noticed that people are becoming more unemotionally present or aware of others, especially when using their mobile devices? Some use them as a distraction and have little time and patience for personal connection.

Whilst in India and the US, I experienced people having a more easy-going attitude. Travelling around it felt so easy to connect with people who were open to having a conversation.

Your culture and how you were brought up usually dictates how safe it is to open up, to show vulnerability and express yourself. It relates to how your mind is coded and how your belief system is wired about other people. For example, if you are someone who believes it is easy and fun to speak to others, you will make friends wherever you go.

## Intuition for emotional intelligence

Intuition is a powerful process to improve our emotional intelligence. Daniel Goleman's definition of emotional intelligence states it is about 'understanding one's own feelings, empathy for the feelings of others and the regulation of emotions in a way that enhances living'. When we look at the word intuition, it is split into two – in-tuition. It is about inner tuition, receiving inner guidance from the teacher within us. It's a process that involves both the head and heart. Intuition is like gut instinct, a sense or knowing without words about someone or a situation before it even happens. Intuition can open you up to a sense of deeper clarity and feeling a soul to soul connection with someone. Your intuition arises as a feeling within your body that only you experience, guiding your thoughts to assist you with creative ideas, great decisions, and motivates you into action.

Intuition helps you to access and connect with your higher self. When you're feeling relaxed and **become present and listen** to the messages that you are receiving from that part of you, it is very powerful. For example, have you ever had an instinct, an idea or a feeling inside to spontaneously do something out of the box? The idea is to engage in your emotions and be in a state of flow rather than listening to your mind chatter.

Intuition is like our GPS navigation system (global positioning system). Imagine when you are driving in the car and you type in the destination, it can lead you on a certain path. You may choose to select the fastest route. However, be prepared to be re-routed as there may be some traffic along the way! Are you someone who is constantly rushing to get somewhere? Do you even know where you are headed, or do you rely on someone else for directions? Have you ever driven your car and arrived at someplace else than you had planned?

I share the following story in the hope that it may help you to STOP and reflect for a moment. Back in 2010, whilst driving to work, I went to slow my car down and my brakes failed. I hadn't been listening to my intuition or paying attention to the signs. My mind and emotions were pre-occupied leading up to the accident. Thankfully, I'm alive and that incident led me to decide I wanted to start a new life.

Just like the GPS we need to navigate our lives, to become present in the moment and listen, re-adjust and be flexible to being re-directed, so we discover something wonderful. Have you noticed when you have followed your gut, you may have found some hidden treasures along the way?

Unfortunately, some of us have lost the natural ability to trust our intuition and rely heavily on GPS, especially with google maps in these modern times. Just think back to how you managed to get around without GPS or devices before.

Now let's look at times when you may not have listened to your intuition. What happened then? Maybe something didn't feel right or wasn't working out as planned. It could be people, places, situations, or the environment. Have you ever walked into a room and felt the energy didn't feel right and walked straight out? Or perhaps met someone and shook their hand and got a weird vibe from them?

We are all intuitive and can practice to develop and enhance this skill.

### Exercise: Connecting with your intuition

1. Think of a time when you listened to your intuition and you felt aligned. How did things go?

2. Think of a time you when you didn't listen to your intuition. How did you overcome this?

3. What did you learn?

**The art is to feel your way** into living an inspirational life. When we listen to our intuition, it connects us to ourselves and offers some valuable clues about what is going on.

**So how can we practice listening to our intuition regularly and keep aligned when things are constantly changing around us?**

We can't control life or our external circumstances, yet we can choose how we respond to others with our body, mind, and emotions. A simple way to get started is to stop, breathe and connect to your body and feelings. Or you may like to ask yourself what you do right now.

Living an inspirational life requires us to get into alignment with ourselves first before making rash decisions or jumping into something blindly. The best way to get into alignment is to listen to our bodies. The body never lies.

'The body is the barometer of your soul.' – Brandon Bays

For instance, if you are seeking direction about something, ask a question and then breathe into the front of your body. If your body remains relaxed, neutral or easy, feel free to take the action needed. If your breath catches, or you feel uneasy, do not take the action. The Body Barometer process developed by Brandon Bays, which I have used with many clients, can further assist you when you are at a crossroads in life, and need clarity to decide.

**Exercise: Body Barometer Process**

First, think of an issue you need to resolve or make a decision on. It could be as simple as going to a party or on a date. Maybe you have been asked to take on a certain opportunity.

Get yourself in a comfortable space and position. You might like to read the exercise below prior to doing this. Then close your eyes. Start by taking a nice deep breath in and out.

Now bring the issue to your mind's eye ...

Imagine you are standing at the top of a road and there are two paths in front of you, one to left and one to the right. Now imagine the left path is as if you don't move forward with your issue. Start walking down that path. How do you feel in your body? Notice your breathing and heartbeat. Just become fully aware. Make a mental note of how it feels and the thoughts that are running through your head.

Now shake it out and come back to neutral and stand at the top of the road again... Take a nice deep breath in and out. This time you are going to take the path to the right. Bring your mind's eye to the issue again. This path is as if you decide to take action to resolve your issue. Just start walking down the right path. How does that feel in your body? Notice your breathing, your heartbeat. Stay connected and take note of what comes up. Now when you are ready open your eyes. You may want to sip some water.

Repeat this process a couple of times if you didn't initially get clarity and remember it takes practice to come into alignment and listen to the body.

You may discover that by using your body as a barometer your ability to trust yourself is strengthened and you can use discernment to assess situations rather than pushing against them. It provides a better indication of what feels important and true to you. When you make decisions that are more aligned to your values, you feel good. Your body will give you feedback as an energetic signal, possibly a feeling in your gut or a tingling sensation followed by a thought.

What came up for you in the process? What did you decide? When you practice becoming present to your intuition, you will learn to allow spirit to guide you to new people, opportunities and places.

Now that you understand the basics of intuition, you can strengthen the connection with your heart to build up your emotional muscle.

## Connect with the heart of who you truly are

Your heart attempts to match with the energy that surrounds you; it adjusts to the frequency. For example, when we hear music or are dancing, we come into rhythm with that energy. The same is true with our connection to the energy frequency of people in our lives.

---

### Exercise: Quick Coherence Technique

A simple technique developed by Heartmath brings your heart and brain into a more aligned state to experience a flow of more positive emotional states.

Practise the exercise for 5 minutes and then notice how you feel. (You can have your eyes either open or closed.)

**Step 1 Heart focus** – shift your attention from your head down into the centre of your heart and maintain your focus there.

**Step 2 Heart focus breathing** – inhale breath through the heart, exhale breath back through the area of the heart.

**Step 3 Heart Feeling** – now think of a time when you felt grateful for something in your life, or love and compassion for someone. Keep breathing in and out from the centre of your chest, whilst thinking about that time and feeling those feelings.

---

### How to release and balance emotions

Every experience has energy and emotions attached to it. You can't change your past experiences, yet you can clear any associated negative emotions. This heals the past and moves you into a state of presence.

> **What if you could open into the vast infinite field of love and peace that already exists within you?**

## Emotional awakening

After leaving my corporate job and travelling to India in 2010, I had a profound emotional awakening, wherein I did not stop crying for almost 4 weeks and lost nearly 10kgs in weight. It led me to the realisation that as part of the spiritual and emotional journey, people need to understand that all emotional energy that exists tends to come rushing to the surface when the timing is right to release it. This energy just wants to be liberated and brought into the space for healing. However, it comes with an old vibration and a reminder of old memories, experiences or perspectives that you may have had in the past. I couldn't believe the amount of emotional baggage I was carrying.

The body remembers everything! It may come through as panic or fear or experiencing a 'dark night of the soul'. The emotions can leave us feeling overwhelmed if we don't know how to handle them. We may try to push them away or tell them to go away. However, they are like children and remain with us. Instead the invitation is to learn to accept them, to turn towards the emotions and enter into a dialogue. Engage with what is showing up in that space, from a place of surrender, compassion, patience and integrate them into a new way of being.

When our emotions are seen and validated, it brings a stillness and presence. We become much lighter and more loving. Our thoughts work in the same way. Just welcome them and, above all, be kind to yourself.

### Exercise: Releasing emotions – letting go!

A very powerful and easy way to release emotions is to write a letter and express all of your unexpressed thoughts and emotions, letting go of the people and situations that no longer serve you. The emotion moves out of your heart and into your hands and is transformed as you write the letter. Just allow your emotions to come out whilst doing this exercise. They are coming up for freedom. Then burn the letter safely with fire, an effective transformer of energy.

Next write a second letter expressing gratitude for all the lessons learned and visualising how much better your life will be now. It's best to do these exercises on the same day for maximum healing.

## Inviting emotions: time for tea

*When I felt misunderstood or my partner was not being supportive, I would go through the following process. Instead of suppressing my feelings, I learned the art of welcoming them. I would invite them in, treating them like friends visiting me, greeting them with an open heart. I would sit and have a cup of tea with them, just observing, acknowledging and allowing the emotions to come up. I would communicate that it was safe to feel my emotions, to sit through the pain and meet it with love and compassion. This helped to dissolve them much faster. I felt much lighter in my body and the tea was comforting afterward. This is something I had to practice regularly for some time as it did not come naturally at first. I now honour my emotions by accepting and welcoming them freely.*

## Daily Practice: Emotional mood tracker

In order to change your emotions, you need to change your perception or action around them. Use your journal so that you can keep a track of your emotions and moods, noting how you are dealing with them.

1. Check in with your emotions each morning and before you go to bed.

2. Name how you feel and rate this on a scale of 1 to 10 – where 1 is not happy and 10 is very happy. Keep a record of this in your journal.

3. Notice which emotions you spend most of your time in. It could be a mixture depending on which activities and people you engage with.

4. Acknowledge your feelings and mood and allow yourself to release them.

5. Then monitor them again on a scale of 1 to 10.

Evaluation helps you keep track of where you are and is best reviewed on a weekly basis. With practice it will get much easier to connect with your emotions. The more aware you become, the more you will be able to notice patterns to be dissolved.

## Welcoming fear

*'The spiritual journey is the unlearning of fear and the acceptance of love back into our hearts.' – Marianne Williamson*

The gateway to love is to feel your fear and move through it. You have two choices when faced with fear; either you forget everything and run, or **face everything and rise**. The choice is yours. The best way to deal with any form of fear is to face it, sit still, feel the feelings, tap into your subconscious and trust this will bring into your awareness a deeper need or desire.

## Being vulnerable is powerful

Sometimes just allowing yourself or someone else to be vulnerable can be deeply healing. In some relationships, it can be hard to open up or even feel safe to do so, as it may be seen as a sign of weakness or bring up fears of being judged. Vulnerability can show up creating a lack of confidence or reminding you of experiences where you might have been rejected or failed at something. You may have been conditioned early on in life to be strong by your parents or other caregivers. For example, when a parent tells you to stop crying, wipe your tears and be a strong girl/boy, it sends a message to the brain that it is not safe to express. There are many experiences that may have caused you to hide out, just like this.

Both men and women use many different tactics to shut out their emotions or wear a false mask. However, there is great strength in being vulnerable. It not only makes you feel lighter, but also opens you up to experiences that bring joy, purpose and love into your life, allowing your authenticity to shine through. It can be a humbling experience to share from an open heart, and gives others permission to do the same.

**Harmonising your emotions**

A simple and powerful Japanese technique called Jin Shin Jyutsu was founded by Master Jiro Murai after he was diagnosed with a terminal illness. This is an ancient energy healing art that I have used with many clients to upgrade their level of self-care and bring balance and harmony to their emotions. There is much to learn from this technique so here I will be focusing on the hands and fingers only.

We all have energy meridians that run through our body; the fingers connect to different emotions that are associated with the major organs. For example, when we worry, we tend to get headaches or digestion issues, which is connected to our stomach and spleen. When we 'try-to', for example, trying too hard or pushing against something to happen, it is connected to our heart and also effects the small intestine.

**Worry** – Thumb (stomach/spleen)

**Fear** – Forefinger (kidney/bladder)

**Anger** – Middle Finger (gall bladder/ liver)

**Sadness/Grief** – Ring Finger (lung/ large intestine)

**Trying-to (Pretense)** – Little Finger (heart /small intestine)

**Balance, Equilibrium** – Centre of palm

The different emotions are illustrated in the diagram below. The easy way to remember this sequence starting with the thumb is to think of **Clear Worry F-A-S-T.**

Anger
Fear
Sadness
Trying-to
(Pretense)

Clear Worry
F-A-S-T

Worry

Equilibrium

---

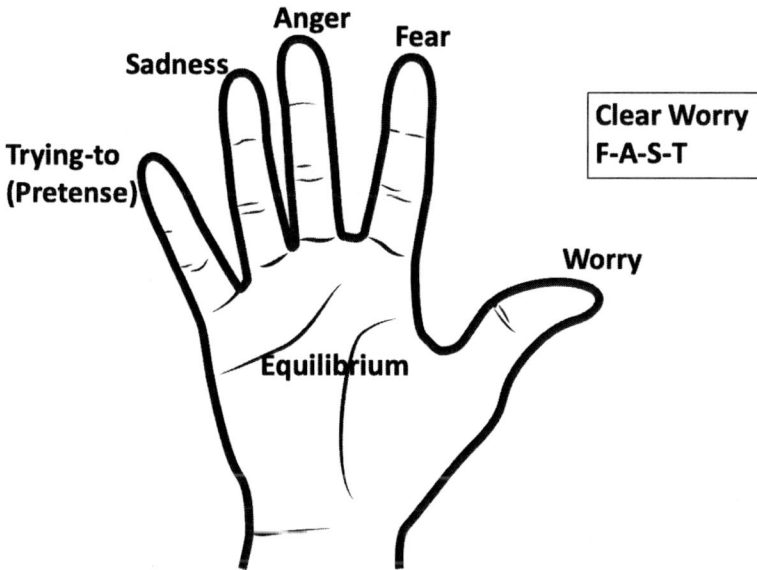

**Daily Practice: Harmonising finger holds**

The great thing about this practice is that you can do this almost anywhere – when you are travelling, in a meeting or watching TV. The best time to do this is when relaxed, so consider doing this whilst meditating or at bedtime. When you are lying down ready for sleep, just hold your fingers, breathe and notice how you may start to drift off into a deep sleep.

Wrap the fingers of one hand around your thumb and hold it lightly for at least 2 minutes. You can hold for longer; just feel into the fingers intuitively. Then move onto the next finger, holding on again for a few minutes. You may begin to feel connected to your pulse; notice if it is strong or weak. Take some deep breaths. You may notice yourself beginning to calm down. Complete one hand and then swap to the other. The final step is to hold the centre of your palm with the fingers of the opposite hand and just breathe in and out. With practice, you will feel a shift in your energy levels and notice a feeling of equilibrium and peace.

---

115

## How can I be in love and stay true to myself?

*'I love because my love is not dependable on the object of love. My love is dependant of my state of being. So, whether the other person changes, becomes different, turns from friend to foe, does not matter. Because my love was never dependant on the other person. I simply love.'* – Osho

Human emotion is a strong aspect of being human. We have a choice to consciously become aware of and select our emotions in each given moment. The more we try to control or possess another through our emotions in our love relationships, the harder it will become to relate to them. When we come from a place of unconditional love for another, our emotions tend to feel less caught up, so we feel more at peace within.

Love transforms our negative emotions and allows us to come into balance with who we are at the core of our being.

*Attachment is the very opposite of love. Love says I want you to be happy. Attachment says I want you to make me happy.*

Have you noticed when you are in love and happy, people want to be around you? Notice your thoughts, words and surroundings that create happiness. When you become unconditionally loving and love flows effortlessly, there is no attachment to anyone or anything.

When you try to be loving yet you are not feeling so, and instead you feel anger, hate and fear, notice who is no longer around you. When people around you appear to be negative, how can you be more loving?

When you stop becoming dependant on another for love, and instead focus on your state of being to keep your emotions in balance, you can become more aware in your relationships and start loving and being true to yourself. You become emotionally detached in a healthy way. The feelings of love, compassion, happiness, joy, peace and bliss come from you when you are in this state. The love flows from within effortlessly.

There is always more you can do to master your emotions, especially if you are dealing with deeper issues in your relationships. For maximum results, it is recommended to work with either a relationship coach or a trained healing practitioner.

**"**

> What type of emotions do you want to experience in your relationships?

**"**

# Chapter 6

# Harmony Bridge

---〜〜〜---

*'The world exists as you perceive it. It is not what you see, it is how you see it. It is not what you hear but how you hear it. It is not what you feel, but how you feel it.' – Rumi*

In this chapter, you will learn how to **bridge the barriers to conflict** and deal with stress, understand your **behaviour** and **expand on a physical level to create more harmony**, love and peace in your relationships.

To imagine harmony, think of musical notes coming together in an orchestrated way to create a pleasing sound to the ears. Harmony is where you want things to flow and work well together, to come to a mutual agreement. As Mahatma Ghandi said, **'happiness is when what you think, what you say and what you do are in harmony'**. Harmony is coming into a beautiful balance of all four energetic bodies – mental, emotional, physical and spiritual.

**"**

> **How might your relationship conflicts be more harmonious if you approach them with greater understanding, mindfulness and kindness?**

**"**

## Bridging barriers to conflict

Each person has a different background, set of beliefs and values and enters into a relationship with their unique perception of seeing, feeling and hearing the world through their own eyes and model of the world. When our perceptions clash in relationships we often encounter conflict.

When you avoid conflict to keep the peace, you start a battle inside yourself. Instead you can use conflict as an opportunity to strengthen your relationships.

The client case below demonstrates how avoiding conflict can impact you from having authentic relationships.

---

### Coming into harmony

*A client of mine learnt from an early age that it was not safe to communicate her views or express anger, otherwise someone would get hurt. She had learned this from watching her parents fighting. Instead she would avoid these angry confrontations by trying to maintain harmony and order in her life, often ignoring her own needs. This later affected the way she would engage in relationships, as she would withhold her emotions and internalise them. She later leaked out feelings of resentment and anger onto others. I could see how this behaviour was preventing her from having real trust, love and connecting authentically in relationships. Through our sessions she was able to breakthrough her barriers and learn how to express herself in much healthier ways. This enabled her to become more assertive, resolve conflict, speak her truth and create harmonious relationships.*

---

Let's look at how you can resolve issues and learn to respect and embrace differences to bridge harmony and create more happiness, love and peace in your relationships.

## Why can't we see eye to eye?

When you experience conflict through anger or confrontational behaviour, you may notice your natural response is to either shut down, try to calm the person down or confront them, all of which are not very helpful. Having seen many cases like this, I've learnt that the root cause of anger is usually connected to the childhood memories of not feeling heard, seen or significant to others due to unmet needs.

The problem can further escalate if there are two people in a relationship who are both driven by significance and express anger in a defensive way. It can bring about power struggles and feelings of negativity.

Repressing anger could also eventually result in having violent outbursts. When you feel anger, the adrenal glands flood the body with stress hormones. The brain pushes blood away from the gut towards the muscles, in preparation for physical exertion. The heart rate speeds up and a rush of hormones, including adrenaline creates a surge of energy strong enough to take 'vigorous action'. Through this process, a reaction has been ingrained into our body to protect us from possible danger.

Anger is not a bad thing if expressed in the right way. It can help you to move out of heavy or stuck emotions such as sadness and hopelessness. There are empowering ways to release anger.

---

### Exercise: Breaking free of anger

So how can you break free of anger?

We will now dive deeper into what may be beneath the anger so that you can understand how patterns play out and how to break free from them. Start by answering the following questions in your journal:

- What makes you angry or upset?

- When was the last time you got angry?

- How do you respond in anger?

- What is this anger teaching you about yourself?

**3 simple tips to manage anger:**

1. When you notice yourself getting angry, sit down! This not only lowers your heart rate, but also calms the nervous system. Count to ten and take some deep breaths! This

---

is extremely powerful. It not only changes your physical state but stabilises your body and mind, which connect to your emotions. It also gives you a chance to collect your thoughts.

2. Take a piece of paper and write down your angry thoughts. Get them all out on paper and release them. For more impact and energetic release, burn the letter, tear it up or flush it down the toilet. If you feel courageous, you could even write a letter outlining what you have been holding onto with another. Then give it to them so they understand how you feel. This allows them to reflect and respond rather than getting into a heated argument. I recommend you processing your emotions first though, so that it may lead to having an open conversation, incorporating forgiveness and creating harmony in your relationship.

3. A far more effective way to express your anger, rather than taking it out on others, is to take a cushion and use it as a punch bag. Imagine releasing the anger as you do this. It's a powerful way to physically release from your body and mind. At first gentler emotions may come to the surface; especially if you have been repressing your anger. It's important to embrace these rather than keep venting.

## Arguments

*'The most profound personal growth happens in the throes of conflict, when you are angry, afraid and frustrated, when you are doing the same old thing and suddenly realise you have a choice'* – *Vironika Tugaleva*

All relationships experience conflict at some time or another. It's normal and a sign that it's time to go deeper with a willingness to understand yourself, so that you can relate from a space of empathy, heartfelt love and appreciation. Dealing with conflict allows you to experience growth and learning through the process so that your soul can evolve to then next level.

Whilst it is important to start identifying what you are arguing about, arguments usually stem from a deeper need to feel love and connection. Small arguments are quite healthy and very common between most people. They help to clear the air and get unwanted feelings off your chest. It can be amusing, especially if there is some healthy banter involved. Arguments can bring passion back into a romantic relationship. For example, have you ever had a partner say that they love it when you get angry or you look hot when you get angry? You can't stay angry for long as this is a pattern break, aiming to break tension and bring some lightness to the situation. Anger can re-ignite chemistry and help move things forward.

There are much better approaches to resolving disagreements than through arguing. Take a moment to think about a challenging relationship and reflect in your journal. Ask yourself:

- 'Is this argument going to matter in a month or a year?'

- 'Is the problem significant enough to impact the relationship as a whole or is something that can be resolved?'

- 'Is the argument more important than the relationship?'

The solution is to train yourself to stop engaging in unproductive arguments that only weaken relationships. Don't try to be right just to prove a point. **Encourage conscious communication** and create the right environment to allow for openness by being transparent and honest. Deal with things as they arise in the moment, instead of letting them fester. This can greatly reduce the need for arguments.

Also note that arguments can happen before you even realise, so learning to apply the powerful tools in this book will assist you to be prepared and choose a different approach. If you do happen to get into a heated argument, take the needed time and space out to give yourself a chance to calm down. Think through how to respond instead of reacting to the other person.

## Perception is projection

*Your perception of me is a reflection of you. My reaction to you is an awareness of me.*

Are you someone who naturally looks for faults in others or what could go wrong? Or are you someone who looks for the good in others and each situation? Did you know that whatever quality you perceive about another, whether that is they are kind, disrespectful or loving, resides within you? It is reflected straight back. Yet, when people tell me the other person is really arrogant and I ask them if they could possibly have those qualities within them, so many say 'No never, not me. I could never be like that!' What if those qualities already exist in you and all you need to do is become aware and come into acceptance to heal them? What you see in others depends mainly on what you are looking for and your perception of people, events and experiences in your life. Once you can understand this powerful concept, your relationships and life will transform for the better.

Instead of projecting certain thoughts and feelings, like blame or hate, look at others through the lenses of love and empathy. If someone has projected something onto you, consider what they may have needed in that moment. Remember that everyone is doing the best they can with the resources they have. This is the key to where most conflict can be dissolved.

## Cause vs. effect

A cause is a reason or event that results in something else happening. There is a connection between them.

If you are going through a difficult time in your relationship or life, and keep attracting arguments or things are not working out for you, it's a result of your thinking. You're looking for everything that is wrong in your relationship or that situation. That is the reason you may continue to face challenges which cause you to be at effect. Instead, look at what is causing you to go into a negative state. What you focus on expands. Where is your focus and what is the meaning you are giving it? Are you in cause or effect?

**Conflict messages**

Some interesting research I came across by psychologist Dr. John Gottman says that there are four conflict messages that can predict whether a couple stay together or get divorced. These are contempt, criticism, defensiveness and stonewalling. All of these should be avoided if you want more harmony in your relationships.

Here are some examples of how you can recognise them playing out in a relationship.

**Contempt** is the most destructive behaviour as it leads to more conflict. Nowadays there are other terms used to describe this such as gaslighting and narcissist behaviours, which include a need for superiority or needing to be better than the other by putting them down. These behaviours create a lack of trust, empathy and respect for others causing hurt and trauma.

**Criticism** is where you look to find fault in the other. It is an expression of disapproval about someone's personality or character that can feel like a personal attack. Instead, accept responsibility and take the other person's perspective into consideration.

**Defensiveness** never solves the problem and can instead make matters worse. It can feel like a back and forth match to prove who is right. It's a form of self-protection where no one actually wins.

**Stonewalling** is withdrawing from the relationship, whether it is in terms of information, physical or emotional energy to cause a disconnect. Usually when one person gets upset or has an opposing view about a certain issue, they react by creating distance and withdrawing their attention and affection. Usually men behave in this way to avoid their emotions. However, this isn't healthy and causes internal conflict. Some behaviours include expressing frustration in passive aggressive ways. For example, slamming doors, or huffing behind a newspaper.

It is best to address issues when they arise, so that you can understand how to resolve them together. The solution is to stop arguing, or take an agreed break for 20 minutes to give each other space to calm down before resuming any conversation.

A simple shift in focus that can help turnaround conflict is to observe your language. Become responsible for your feelings, thoughts and actions rather than blaming the other. For instance, instead of saying 'you made me feel...', or 'you always do...', say, 'I felt... when this happened'. Make it about the situation and not the person. Remember, nobody is responsible for making you feel a certain way, unless you allow them to. They did not put the feelings inside you. They were there all along, so take ownership!

Here is a story of a client who experienced contempt. She used the approaches above to express her feelings and break free.

### Freedom from contempt

I worked with a woman who felt disrespected in her relationship. She shared how her partner would use sarcasm and his body language (by doing things such as eye-rolling) especially when they were out together in public. He would also correct her sentences as a way to put her down. She felt worthless. After some coaching sessions, she realised the behaviour had more to do with him and stopped taking it personally. She was then able to have a conversation with him to express how she felt using 'I' statements. He was not open to understand her, instead telling her that she was 'over-reacting as usual' and started twisting things around. In such cases of contempt, this kind of language is used to detract from the person, making them question themselves. The sessions helped her evaluate the relationship as a whole and she decided to leave. This was a way to honour her self-respect and maintain her sanity, opening herself up to a healthier relationship. An awareness of self-growth was more important than accepting his behaviour.

As you can see conflict can lead to many consequences if not resolved properly. The same issues will re-surface time and time again until you learn the lessons they have to offer. Whether it is internal or external conflict, it leaves you feeling powerless, emotionally drained and stressed. When you truly love someone, you can still have a healthy balance of conflict and a choice in how you respond. More importantly, it is about recognising the behavioural signals early on in a relationship so that you are able to resolve things before they begin to fester.

---

### Exercise: Harmony Bridge

To help you bridge the gap to creating harmony in your relationships, write down the answers to the following:

**Awareness Bridge**

1. Become aware of your triggers. What are they?

2. What is upsetting you?

3. What are you arguing about?

4. What is causing you to respond negatively?

5. Notice what happens to your body language. Where do you hold tension and what is happening to your breathing? Is it shallow and constricted? What about your heart rate?

**Acceptance Bridge**

1. What can you accept in this moment?

2. What can't you accept?

3. Are you able to accept it if they never change?

4. How can you respond to achieve the desired outcome?

**Action Bridge**

1. What needs to be expressed?

2. What can't be expressed?

3. What small step can you take to move forward?

---

## Take the stress out of relationships

**Today, why don't you love a little deeper, laugh a little louder, hold the ones you love a little tighter. Because tomorrow is never promised.**

Relationships can cause a great deal of stress if not managed properly.

There is both good and bad stress. Good stress is where we feel pumped up with adrenalin and oxytocin (the body's happy hormone). When oxytocin is released in the body it keeps us motivated and focused on doing what we love.

Here we will be looking at what happens in our bodies when we have bad stress and particularly when conflict happens.

How do you respond to conflict? Are you someone who avoids it or do you become defensive? How does your body respond? Does it go into fight, freeze or flight mode? This response is caused by a biochemical reaction in the body's chemistry for both humans and animals. It enables them to deal with perceived danger by providing sufficient energy, adrenalin and cortisol (the stress hormone) to either go into a fight, flight or freeze reaction in the body. Unfortunately, when the stress hormone is released, it can lead to retaining weight (amongst other side effects), hence it's key to manage your stress levels if you want to manage your weight!

Anxiety and stress are very common. Once you recognise that these emotions are not at the core of who you truly are, you come back into alignment with yourself, raising your energetic vibration. Learning how to deal with stress reduces these symptoms so that you can feel happy and have more success and harmony in your relationships. We all have the power within to heal ourselves.

**3 simple ways to deal with stress:**

1. **Meditation and mantras**

   Meditation is practiced more widely now than ever before and is excellent for relaxation and stress reduction. It doesn't require any special equipment and there is no medication involved. It's a mind-body complimentary medicine that can be practised almost anywhere, whether sitting at home, commuting, whilst out walking or at work. For people who are beginners, I would suggest starting off by finding a quiet setting where you will not be disturbed. Schedule in the time and keep distractions to a minimum, i.e., switch off your phone, laptop or television.

I have been meditating since childhood without even realising it. My mother was very spiritual and would arrange for people to come together at our home and sing mantras and bhajans regularly. The word mantra can be broken down into two parts: 'man', which means mind, and 'tra', which means transport or vehicle. In other words, a mantra is an instrument of the mind, a powerful sound or vibration that you can use to enter a deep state of meditation. Mantras help to ease the heart and relax the busy mind. 'Bhajan' means sharing and also refers to any song with a religious, spiritual or devotional meaning. It's free flowing, normally lyrical and has a soothing and healing effect on the mind, body and spirit.

Meditating, chanting or prayer in groups can heighten your awareness and bring you into a greater state of presence, bliss and love as everyone has the same intention. The difference is that prayer is when you ask for guidance whilst meditation is where you become still and listen to the guidance within. You can reach a level of oneness and connection, by bringing your awareness and focus to the sounds around you, repeating the sacred mantras over and over again.

In the early days, whilst working my corporate job, I would offer regular meditation classes in my home every week to people who wanted to learn and deepen in their practice. They reported feeling more calm, relaxed, present and able to handle their challenges from a different perspective upon re-entering their own spaces.

Meditation has become a natural way of being for me. It feels more like an open-eyed process, viewing life from a childlike innocence and present awareness. It has allowed more connection and harmony with each moment and person, and more acceptance for everything exactly as it is. It's just a deeper observation of self, life and others, with no addition of anything.

Most people say they don't have time to meditate. However, all it takes is 5 or 10 minutes to sit quietly with yourself, preferably each morning and before you go to bed. With some discipline and practice you will start noticing the effects in your energy levels, focus and capacity to think and be more productive.

## Become aware of the monkey mind

I first became aware of the term 'monkey mind' from reading books about Buddhism and from many spiritual teachers in India. The **'monkey mind'** is a term that refers to the brain being unsettled, restless, or confused. Have you ever watched the behaviour of monkeys? They are very intelligent animals. However, they become easily distracted and can't sit still, jumping from one thing to another. The term made a lot of sense to me! So if you want to get anything done in life, your challenge will be to **quieten the monkey mind,** especially during meditation.

The invitation here is to observe and acknowledge the thoughts that can often escalate into a downward spiral and be the cause of unnecessary drama. The purpose of meditation is not to ignore your thoughts. Instead it is to welcome them and discover what impact they have on your bodies. Everything is inter-connected – your mind, emotions, body and spirit. Where is this feeling in your body? How does it make you feel? When you fully open into your emotions, you tap into a space of inner peace which uplifts your spirit and your purpose for being.

There are many different types of meditation practices; here are some of the simplest ways to get you started:

- **Focused attention** helps keep your mind free from distractions. You can start to practise focusing your attention on a specific object. For example, use a candle, flower or an image of a picture or a painting. Rather than intense concentration, it is more about letting go and relaxing. Focusing on sound is also very powerful. It could be as simple as the wind, traffic, an air conditioner or even the rhythm of your breathing. Just pick one thing.

- **Breathing** is what keeps us alive. Relaxed breathing involves deep breathing using the diaphragm muscles to expand your lungs in an even paced way. This assists in intaking more oxygen, slowing down your breathing and moving you from shallow breathing in your upper chest to deep, relaxed breathing. You can start by breathing in to the count of four and exhaling out to the count of four, repeating for as long as necessary.

Relaxed breathing and practicing meditation can help you to ease tension, gain a new perspective on your situation, increase self-awareness, improve your patience and tolerance and help you focus on being present when communicating with others. This is turn helps you balance your energy and achieve clarity in your thinking, therefore inspiring you to create new ideas and make better decisions.

2. **Laughter**

You've heard the saying 'laughter is the best medicine' and indeed it is. People who laugh together, and have a sense of humour and fun, have a stronger bond. Did you know that laughter produces more oxygen and helps you to breathe, also releasing oxytocin into the brain?

Having a sense of humour is the number one quality people look for when choosing a partner. Humour is becoming the new hot!

To ease any stress, think of a moment that made you laugh. Go back and re-live that event. You can watch funny videos, comedy and movies or listen to something that makes you laugh.

One of the best ways to start laughing is to watch someone else laughing or attend a laughter class. Calling up friends or family and reminiscing over silly times can make you feel wonderful. It really works!

Think of situations in your relationships, that made you laugh out loud. This helps to lighten the mood and connect you to your creativity and joy.

3. **Physical Exercise**

Exercise has so many health benefits including managing physical and mental stress, releasing happy endorphins into the bloodstream, boosting brain power, helping to control addictions and reduce cravings to substances, increasing relaxation and aiding a better night's sleep.

Physical exercise is an excellent mood booster. If you want to improve your mindset, or improve your intimate connection and sex life, then do some exercise. Like the saying goes if you 'don't move it or use it, you lose it'! Regular physical activity may enhance arousal for women. Men who exercise regularly are less likely to have problems with erectile dysfunction than men who don't exercise.

The good news is it only takes 20 minutes of exercise a day to make you feel physically better, increase your energy and creativity levels, add years to your life and make you look younger and keep your body weight maintained, which boosts your confidence and self-esteem.

Some simple suggestions would be:

- Walking in nature

- Running

- Cycling

- Yoga

Create space for fun times spent with each other. Find a fun activity either you or both of you like doing together or sign up to a class, i.e., dancing, hiking etc.

---

**Daily Practice: Get active**

Pick one activity and do it for 20-30 minutes a day. Make it a part of your daily routine. Journal how your energy level feels before and after. You could also weigh yourself regularly at the same time every day and assess your results after 30 days.

---

**Physical pain: The body never lies**

Are you aware that the body contains some 50 trillion cells, and each is full of emotions and memories?

The body is very intelligent and has a way of remembering every memory and experience. Have you ever wondered how physical pain shows up in the body? Where does it come from? The body is a mirror of your mind. As you worry, your body reflects it. Many people report having physical symptoms due to their relationship issues – back ache, chest pain, migraine, stomach upset, etc. Of course, nobody wants to feel pain or experience these symptoms, right? I'm not suggesting you just pop some pills and get a temporary fix for the pain. Instead how would you really like to get to the root cause of the pain and clear it?

The body just wants your attention. It's sending a message that you've not been listening. In some cases, the pain can get worse and even become debilitating; it may eventually make you physically slow down or force you to stop altogether. The body can go into breakdown mode when it feels ignored and create internal conflict and illness. Learning to nurture your body with respect and love can help you grow through the discomfort.

---

### *Fear of success*

*A client was experiencing a lot of discomfort with her kidney stones. She was on several medications, yet the pain persisted and she became unable to focus. When I sat with her, I noticed she had a lot of resistance to start with. Gradually, she tuned into her body and sat with the pain. With my guidance, she discovered that the root cause of this conflict lay in the fear of her being successful and not wanting to disappoint her mother. Applying the bridge to love method, enabled her to connect to her emotions, release guilt and get relief from the discomfort. For the first time, she managed to have a heartfelt conversation with her mother and understood what was driving her control issues. Her pain disappeared and she was able to continue running a successful business without feeling pain or pressure.*

---

People often use pain or illness as a way to get attention from others. This is known as a secondary gain. It's when you may not be feeling loved or getting the desired attention from your partner and others, so you manifest illness to receive the quality time, care and love you desire from them. This usually links back to unmet needs as a child.

If this pattern continues over a period of time, it can fail and cause others to move away from you rather than bringing you closer. It also makes you co-dependant on another for happiness, instead of seeking it inwardly.

Another behaviour to avoid pain and discomfort is distraction, where you choose to carry on as normal with your daily routine. Some distractions may include an excess of cleaning, watching TV, checking social media, or eating. It's doing anything else but sitting still and connecting with the body.

**Exercise: Listening to the body**

Ask yourself, in which ways do you distract yourself from pain?

Take a moment now to just stop and become aware. Listen carefully to your body and the sensations that you are feeling.

If you notice any tension, what is it trying to tell you?

What does the pain need from you right now?

Just stop and listen. The answers may just surprise you.

### Veena's vertigo

*Veena came to see me as she was experiencing dizzy spells which started off as headaches and gradually got worse. Her GP had diagnosed her as having vertigo. She felt nauseous and unable to function normally, despite taking medication. I asked her when these symptoms had started. She broke down and told me that it was when she discovered her husband was having an affair with one of the neighbours in their block. She felt embarrassed and just couldn't get her head around it. My knowledge on how the body parts and physical ailments are connected allowed me to explain from a healing perspective how vertigo links to the thinking mind and a fear of not being able to look at the present situation. I guided her to simply listen to her body and the message she was receiving. Veena was able to clear her issues at the root and eventually regained balance. Months later she called me and told me she had come to terms with her relationship situation and had decided to leave her husband and start her own business.*

## Extramarital affairs

One reason for the increased divorce rates is that extramarital affairs are on the rise across the world. Extramarital affairs can occur when you have lost sexual connection, compassion and understanding with your partner. It can be natural to feel attraction for another if those qualities are no longer present in your relationship. An extramarital affair can bring with it the excitement of newness, secrecy, emotional connection, a strong sense of desire, intimacy and passionate sex.

Unfortunately, it also brings with it heightened unbalanced emotions, and feelings of being addicted, attached and vulnerable. Affairs take up a lot of mental energy due to keeping secrets, telling lies and remembering the truth. It causes stress, anxiety and shame. It's a big risk as you could lose everything just for that moment of temporary passion, happiness, and connection.

Affairs can also present an opportunity to re-evaluate your relationship and each other's emotional needs. With the right guidance and tools, this experience can produce a breakthrough in communication and understanding, leading to rekindled love and a deeper connection.

Sometimes, however, it may be necessary to break away from the relationship if there is no longer any respect, love or trust. If the relationship feels toxic and is draining your energy and joy, or if there is physical violence or an addiction issue that is out of control, it is best to seek professional help.

## Healing the body with colours and sounds

When you learn to understand the language of energy and the impact it has on the body, it will enhance your life on many levels.

Did you know that colours and sound can have a profound healing effect on the body, creating harmony and balance? This is because there is a direct link to colours and sound from the body's energy centres (the 7 chakras). There are many more chakras in the energy system, however we will just focus on the main 7 in this book.

'Chakra' is a Sanskrit word which means 'wheel of light'. Each of these energy centres holds a different vibrational frequency, associated colour and meaning. When you tune into each of these frequencies, visualising and sensing colours and the associated sounds, it can help you balance the energy of each chakra. This is not only beneficial for your wellbeing but is also the only way to unite the individual soul with the universal soul.

## The 7 chakras – The body's energy centres

Starting from the top of the head and working down to the base of the spine:

**The 7th chakra – crown chakra (sahasrara In Sanskrit) meaning thousand petaled.** Located at the top of your head.

**Colour: pure white.** It's where we are connected to our higher selves, universe or pure consciousness.

**Sound: 'hum'**

**Out of harmony:** Unable to let go of anxiety and fear. Depressed and unsatisfied. Unable to imagine cosmic unity.

**In harmony:** In unity with cosmic divine.

**The 6th chakra – third eye chakra (ajna in Sanskrit).** Located in the centre of the forehead, between the eyes.

**Colour: deep indigo.** Represents our insight, vision and wisdom. This can be activated through practising meditation, yoga and other spiritual practices.

**Sound: 'ksham'**

**Out of harmony:** Rejection of spiritual aspects. Focus on intellect and science. Only sees surface meaning. Afraid of intuition.

**In harmony:** Awareness of spirituality. Invites intuition and connection with the divine.

**The 5th chakra – throat chakra (vishuddha in Sanskrit)**

**Colour: light blue.** It is associated with our expression and the centre of communication with others. This chakra can become blocked if we do not express our truth with others. Women can develop thyroid issues if this chakra becomes blocked. Associated with purification.

**Sound: 'ham'**

**Out of harmony:** Unable to find expression. Fearful of being judged and rejected. Afraid of silence.

**In harmony:** Balance of expression, silence and speech. Listening to the inner voice. Singing, humming, chanting and speaking with love.

### The 4th chakra – heart chakra (anahata in Sanskrit)

**Colour: green.** This is our love centre and the bridge to connection and compassion between the 3 upper and 3 lower chakras.

**Sound: 'yam'**

**Out of harmony:** Love given is not sincere. You cannot accept love given by others.

**In harmony:** Exudes a feeling of wholeness. Tolerance and acceptance of life and relationships. Balance of the material and spiritual worlds.

In order to evolve, we need to work on the lower 3 chakras which govern our security, safety and relationship to others. This is where we are externally focused and work towards opening and expanding the top 3 to create greater states of bliss, expression and clarity and become into oneness with ourselves and connect to the divine. **The heart is the bridge.**

### The 3rd chakra – solar plexus (manipura in Sanskrit). Located above the navel.

**Colour: yellow.** This governs wellbeing and the relationship we have with ourselves and the outer world. When out of balance it can leave us feeling disconnected.

**Sound: 'ram'**

**Out of harmony:** Not trusting natural flow. Great need for material security.

**In harmony:** Feeling of wholeness, inner calm and peace. Inner acceptance of others. Balance of spiritual and material worlds.

**The 2ⁿᵈ chakra – sacral chakra (svadhishthana in Sanskrit).** Located just below the navel in the lower abdomen.

**Colour: orange.** It is connected with our emotional body, sexual organs, sensuality, fertility and creativity. This chakra can become blocked by fear.

**Sound: 'vam'**

**Out of harmony:** Unstable in sexual and emotional matters. Suppresses feelings and natural needs.

**In harmony:** Considerate, kind and friendly approach. Expresses emotions with others at ease. Happily, connected to life.

**The 1ˢᵗ chakra – root chakra (muladhara in Sanskrit).** Located at the base of the spine.

**Colour: red.** It is the chakra for stability and security and getting our basic needs met. It is also where our Kundalini (life force) or fire energy is created. The purpose of Kundalini energy is to awaken our spiritual or higher dimensional frequencies and is connected with the brain and nervous system. This is where we are connected to mother earth, so when out of balance we can feel ungrounded.

**Sound: 'lam'**

**Out of harmony:** Inability to trust nature. Focus on material possessions. Need to satisfy own desires.

**In harmony:** Profound connection and trust in nature. Deep understanding of the ebb and flow of life.

**Daily Practice: Mantra meditation chanting**

**Aum, or Om, is a powerful mantra and considered a primordial sound of the universe in Hinduism.** It is often chanted as a prefix to any mantra. According to some music theorists, when chanted the vibration is 432HZ, which is the frequency at which the universe vibrates. By listening to or repeating the **sound** of 'Aum' we can make a connection to the voice of our own heart and balance our chakras.

Not only does sounding Aum have a calming effect on the body, it also eases any anxiousness you may be feeling. You can chant the other sounds for the specific chakras above too. An alternative to chanting Aum is humming with your mouth closed.

Here's how it works:

1. **Schedule a regular time to practice for around 5 to 10 minutes**

2. **Chant Aum 21 times on repeat, either aloud (this is best) or in your mind**

3. **Chant each mantra slowly, allowing the breath to flow with ease**

4. **Sit still after chanting and notice your energies and the presence**

## Body as a temple of love

When was the last time you really listened to your body? The idea of the body as a temple of love is not a new one. However very few people truly believe this or take care to honour and respect it. In other words, we take our physical bodies for granted. We do not take time to truly pay attention to its signals and engage in meaningful conversation with it.

How is the body really a temple of love? Firstly, the very fact that it was conceived with desire shows its love-based origin. Our body is the temple that houses our soul. It's the only one we have, so all the more reason to treat it as our sacred home and to worship it with love and respect.

It is the absolute seat of love as trillions of cells in our body co-operate and align every second without us even having to think about a thing! It's truly miraculous. Have you ever had to think about where your next breath would come from, or what happens inside you whilst you are sleeping, eating, walking, blinking, etc.? The list of the body's miraculous functions is endless, and it all happens at a subconscious level to keep us alive and healthy!

Just as we do things to keep our life in order, similarly we need to enhance our body's performance so that we have the maximum benefits and can grow old gracefully. Here are a few examples:

1. Nutrition – what you eat and put into your body is who you become. You will notice you don't actually need to eat a lot if you are eating mostly fresh, plant-based foods rather than processed foods and drink plenty of water. Become mindful of the quantity and portion size. When I speak of nutrition, I'm referring not only to food but also the nutrition of thoughts. We must take the upmost care to feed our minds consciously with healthy, loving thoughts, especially when preparing or eating food as these emit a certain energy frequency into the body. What are you feeding your mind and body?

2. Communicating with your body – this may sound a little bizarre to some, however the outcome is incredible. For instance, if you have a headache or some tension in your body, you could place a hand on that area and ask it questions, such as 'What is bothering you?' or 'What do you need right now?' Have a dialogue with that body part. More often than not, you will receive an answer which will give you a major breakthrough.

3. Rest and relaxation – we can only function well if we have balance in our lives. Whilst navigating through our hectic schedules, we must remember to organise some much-needed time for ourselves. When was the last time you stopped and

became more mindful of your pace? When did you last give yourself permission to take a nap, treat yourself to a massage or just quietly meditate?

4. The magic of your body – it all starts with trusting that your body always knows how to heal itself naturally. Sometimes we may complicate things by taking medication and other substances to feel better. It is only when we acknowledge, appreciate and believe in the body's remarkable energy system that we can stay in this temple of love with ease, joy and grace.

Think of a time when you were not feeling so well. How did you treat your body? Do you push yourself to get things done for others out of fear, worry or guilt? Perhaps you go to an unfulfilling job just so that you can pay the bills.

Have you ever noticed how you may get sick just as you are about to go on a vacation or during your time off from work? Why is that? The probable cause is over thinking, not sleeping or eating well, or constantly worrying and pushing yourself to get tasks completed on time. When the body is tired, our immunity levels can become low and we fall sick. Pay attention. Our body responds honestly to what we put into it and how we treat it. If we listen to our body, it will thank us.

> **How are you treating your body as a temple of love?**

**The old healer to his soul**
It's not your back that hurts, but the burden.
It's not your eyes that hurt, but the injustice.
It's not the head that hurts, it's your thoughts.
Not the throat, but what you don't express or say with anger.
Not the stomach hurts, but what the soul does not digest.
It's not the liver that hurts, it's the anger.
It's not your heart that hurts, but love.
And it is love itself that contains the most powerful medicine.
*Ada Luz Marquez*

# Harmony in relationships

## Marriage and divorce

Whilst travelling and working in India for seven years, I witnessed many cultural differences when it came to relationships and understood the concept of arranged marriages. In some places, especially rural villages, many couples didn't get to know one another properly before marriage, as dating was not the norm in the society. Some couples chose to date accompanied by a family member or friend or would meet up in secret.

Some people marry for the wrong reasons with marriages often being carried out to fulfil a duty to the parents, possibly even to keep the family legacy going. For some it is about doing the right thing in the eyes of society, respecting their family's reputation and maintaining social status.

However, nowadays all that is slowly changing. There is more acceptance and openness. Some couples choose their own partners and introduce them to family members before deciding to live together or get married.

I believe that India had good statistics around the durability of marriage at one time. This was driven by the culture and relationship values. However, times have certainly changed given the evolving influence from Western society, social media and the fast growth of the country. I was surprised to learn recently that domestic violence and divorce rates are on the increase. One article in the Times of India, shared that 70% of women are divorced and the number one thing they suffer from is aloneness. They just can't cope as no one taught them to live alone. They were brought up learning how to take care of others, so when they are by themselves they feel unproductive. I have worked with many women in India, empowering them to break free of their inner limitations, and overcome pain so that they feel more self-love, happier and have harmony in their lives.

**There are so many couples out there that don't love each other, yet choose to stay together, and the ones that really do love one another cannot be together.**

### Harmony in marriage

I worked with a housewife in India, whose parents arranged her marriage at a young age. She told me she had little in common with her husband. The relationship was lacking friendship, intimacy and sexual connection. The only reason for intimacy was to conceive children. She became bored and later met a man who she became friends with. He was also married, had children and no real connection with his wife. She told me that the relationship enabled them to fulfil each other's need for companionship, love, understanding and communication They had a deep soul connection between them.

Having seen many such cases like this, I could sense that there was a desire for love and connection, yet sadness that she could not be with someone that she loved due to fear of being abandoned by society. We worked to release the emotion of sadness and fear caused by these thoughts. She let go of the sadness, guilt and self-judgement and realised that everything happens for a reason. She also understood she had the power of choice. I asked her to consider what else she was learning from this situation and she realised she needed to work more on the relationship with herself and what she wanted. Working on herself enabled her to come into acceptance and self-love. She began to notice and appreciate her husband and saw how her thoughts had caused a barrier between them. They started to spend more time together as a family and experienced more happiness and harmony in their marriage.

## Why are people unfaithful in relationship?

I often get asked by clients who have been unfaithful or are being treated unfaithfully why people are unfaithful. This starts when there is a disconnection and lack of open communication. If you have been on the receiving end it can really hurt, and if you are the one being unfaithful it leaves you feeling guilty and full of shame.

## Rebuilding trust

I met a woman who shared with me that she had a wonderful, trusting relationship. She did everything she could to make her partner feel special and was happy as he never stopped her from doing what she wanted. One night she went out with her friends whilst her partner was watching sport on TV at home. They had agreed that he would pick her up when she was ready to come home.

It got late and she didn't want to disturb him so she got a lift home with a friend. To her surprise when she arrived home her partner was chatting and laughing with another woman whom she had not met before. Her heart sank. She felt betrayed just at the sight of them together and ran back out. Through our coaching sessions she learned how to release the feelings of confusion and betrayal and communicate openly about how it made her feel. They managed to clear up any misunderstanding, resolve conflict and rebuild trust to save their relationship.

You may know exactly how this feels. You feel hurt inside. Thoughts can start running through your mind and you may even start to think that it is all your fault. 'I'm not good enough!' 'What does he/she see in them?' 'He/she doesn't love me.' 'I'm not beautiful enough.' The list goes on and the mind goes into a downward spiral with all sorts of thoughts, limiting beliefs and stories creating negative emotions. Recognise that when someone is disloyal it reflects who they are; it's their insecurities, not yours.

Being unfaithful can be subtle. It doesn't just mean kissing, meeting or getting physically involved with another. It could be simple things like flirting or deleting messages from your phone to hide them from your partner. The fact is, people who are unfaithful don't think it's wrong until it happens to them or someone they care about.

Trust isn't simply given in a relationship. It is built up gradually and earned over time. Creating an environment where both can openly express their thoughts and feelings freely, enables relationships to work. When both people feel respected, there is little need to prove your trust.

**How do you deal with jealousy?**

Imagine a situation where someone you are in a relationship with makes you jealous by flirting with someone else. What is your reflex response to this situation? I've asked many people, who came up with the following:

1. they would walk away, ignoring it and acting as if nothing happened

2. they would flirt with someone else to make them jealous

3. they would get into a heated argument, as they've been emotionally triggered and are angry.

There are better ways to deal with jealousy, especially when you start to get emotionally triggered. You can deal with jealousy without playing games that could have harmful effects on the relationship. Did you know it often sends a message to your partner's brain that you are rewarding them for the things that you don't want them to do? This can satisfy their need to feel more significant, rather than becoming aware and wanting to change their behaviour.

The best thing to do is to be honest in an objective way. The more open and honest you are, the more you can turn the relationship around. For example, you could say what you did is really not acceptable and let them know your values. If they truly value you and the relationship they will make amends.

- How have you been a victim of jealousy or compared yourself to others?

- What are your personal values in your relationship?

- How can you start to value yourself better?

## Flowers don't compete

> *'A flower does not think of competing with the flower next to it. It just blooms.'* – *Zen Shin*

Just as flowers don't compete, we can also bloom where we are, regardless of how we perceive others around us. Simply see the goodness in yourself and others. Then you'll complement, not compete with those around you.

# Love beyond pain

**Love is worth more than the pain you will go through.**

Loving beyond pain is where we learn to be comfortable with being uncomfortable. There are going to be times when you will feel immense pain in your relationship for whatever reason; maybe you are not being respected, valued or loved. It's also possible the relationship has outgrown itself or become unhealthy for you. Just know it's natural to go through tough times and part of the growth journey.

A large part of suffering is caused by separation, from yourself, from others, your mind and from source. It's good to acknowledge the pain caused by this, instead of ignoring it. Just don't stay there longer than is needed. There is a saying that **'pain is inevitable but suffering is optional'**. You have a choice to come into oneness with yourself, everything and everyone. Here you will feel a sense of connection. Just know that loving yourself is worth more than the pain you will go through. Use your pain to fuel your light. Not everyone will know your struggle, but soon everyone will know your light.

### How to deal with toxic relationships

Sometimes we may even need to leave a relationship that feels toxic and is not in alignment with our true values. How do you know when a relationship is toxic? It feels like it has outgrown itself. You no longer feel valued and you end up doing things for your partner from a place of fear or obligation. The relationship can feel more toxic the longer you stay there and tolerate the situation. You are no longer growing together. There is a one-sided agenda or a feeling of being manipulated for something that the other wants from you. It starts feeling transactional, even though relationships should never be transactional.

Don't do anything drastic before assessing fully where you are. Take some time to get into stillness and ask yourself some quality questions.

---

**Exercise: How do I know if this relationship is right for me?**

Ask yourself these questions:

1. How does this relationship bring out the best in me? Does it make me feel loved and support my growth?

2. How is this relationship aligned with my values?

3. How is this relationship serving me or not serving me?

4. What am I discovering about myself in this relationship?

---

The reason why so many potential relationships fail is because people feel broken, yet they think a relationship will make them feel better. They hang on to it because it is better than having nothing at all. However, healing your heart requires some isolation and introspection. The problem is most people haven't come to terms with being alone or liking their own company.

The biggest distance between two people is when misunderstandings occur. Relationships can work if both people invest the much-needed time and energy to connect. It requires honest communication, trust and commitment. It also requires you being on your own journey and growing to be a better version of yourself. Growing together requires growing individually. The distance in a relationship doesn't matter if the roots of your relationship are strong enough. If the relationship is worth it, you will both find a way to make it work.

# Love the lessons

### Learn to love when you don't want to

No relationship is ever a waste of time. If it didn't bring you what you wanted, it helps to teach you what you don't want. A simple process that can help you is to list down all the times you have felt hurt, along with the people involved. Then work to release the emotions and come to forgiveness with yourself and others.

If the people in your life left, or you left them, because they were not ready to value you, to be there for you, to love and respect you, let them go. Do not ask for them to be more than they can be in the moment. You don't have to hate them. Remember their contribution to your life as a beautiful gift. Do not ruin them in your mind or grip onto resentment. Instead the invitation is to love them without attachment. **Love the lessons that they came to teach you.** Wish them well every single time you think of them and then let them go. Miss them but do not ache for them to come back. Wish for them to figure themselves out, to grow and learn their own lessons someday. They are on their own journey, which you are not a part of. You have to come to terms with being okay with that. Just send them love and focus on loving yourself.

Love comes to those who still hope after disappointment, who still believe after betrayal, and who still love after they have been hurt. Move past the pain and hurt and be in acceptance. Maybe they weren't the best for you. You are not defined by the experiences you have had in the past. Whatever happened has been and gone. Don't stress about the relationships that didn't work out and the 'could haves'. If it should have been, it would have been. Look back at those times as opportunities for release and much needed healing within. You are much bigger and better than your past. **Keep shining your light on your bright future. Are you ready to love again?**

Every relationship can become 'boring' after you've been together for years, unless you consciously work to sustain it. After all, love isn't a feeling, but a way of being. You commit to love every day, with every ounce of you. It can be challenging and is not always enjoyable.

People tend to quit quickly when it stops being fun and start looking for someone else because the 'spark' has gone. But that's really not how it works. If you want someone to never give up on you and love you unconditionally, then you have to be willing to do the same. You need to work together to come up with new creative ideas to bring back that spark. Be the change you want to see. Give that which you want to receive. If you want honesty, be honest! Learn to love someone when you don't want to, when they aren't easy to deal with, when they're playing hard to love. That takes courage. **Be real in love.**

Most of all, love the lessons and build a bridge of harmony in your relationships by choosing to love over hate, conflict, indifference, ignorance, ego, fear, barriers, and borders. **Choose love over and over and over again.**

# Chapter 7

# Communication Bridge

———— ⌘ ————

*'Between what is said and not meant, and what is meant and not said, most of love is lost.' – Kahil Gibran*

## Bridging barriers to conscious communication

I think the quote above sums up the meaning of communication beautifully. So much of how we communicate in relationships is open to misinterpretation. We often say things that we don't mean; it just comes out without any prior thought. Or we don't have the courage to say what really needs to be said so, in that moment, the love and possibility for connection is lost. There are many reasons why this may happen.

In this chapter you will learn how to **communicate with courage** and **compassion** so that you can **impact and influence others** to feel understood and **get what you need** from your relationships. Have a think about a relationship that is important to you, one you would like to improve upon. **When was the last time you communicated your truth from a place of understanding and love?**

## What is communication?

Quite simply, communication is an exchange of information between individuals through symbols, signs, or behaviour. It is a skill that is learnt from the moment we are born. If you observe a baby, although they cannot speak, they quickly learn that by crying or laughing they can get most of their needs met. Babies are naturally present and live through their feelings rather than thoughts. Similarly, you can tell whether a person is happy or sad just by becoming aware of their emotional state, facial gestures, body language and the tone of their voice.

## Communication model

Below is a model originally developed by *John Grinder* and *Richard Bandler*, that I learned during my NLP (Neuro Linguistic Programming) training. It illustrates the foundation for how we communicate.

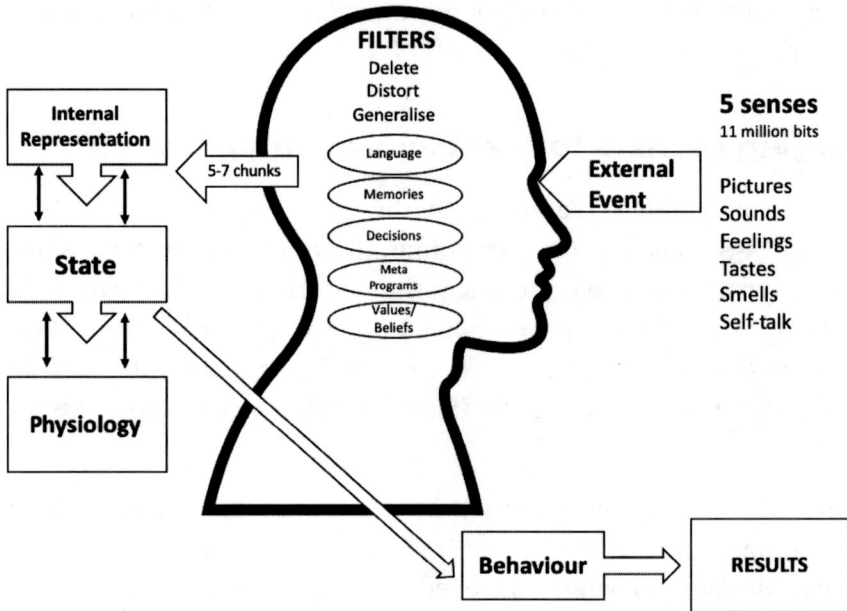

Using the analogy of the brain operating like a computer, we take in approximately 11 million bits of information per second from the external world. This information is received by our five senses in the form of pictures, sounds, feelings, tastes, smells and self-talk. Internally our conscious mind can only process around 134 bits per second into 5 or 7 chunks.

That information is filtered through a process of deleting, distorting or generalising based on your life experiences, decisions, values, beliefs and programming. This then creates the way you see the world, events and people and effects your thoughts, emotions, physiology, behaviours and results in life.

Have you ever noticed that people treat their perceptions differently? Some people have to 'see' a certain relationship between things, whilst others need it explained so they can 'hear it'. Some people have to 'get a grasp or a feeling' for the relationships. This is because we all process information in different ways. This is the essence of the NLP Communication Model.

The take-away point here is that even though we can logically understand how it all works, it's important to observe how you communicate in practice and the impact it has on others and yourself.

## How communication styles affect relationships

Each person has a unique communication style which affects how they interact with others, whether in their personal or professional relationships. Discovering your primary communication style as well as that of others, will help you minimise misunderstandings and frustrations and maximise effective communication. This is less about labelling yourself with a certain style and more about using this information to come into awareness of yourself, so that you can learn to grow and contribute to your relationships. I cover more about communication at the experiential level in my coaching sessions and programmes.

There are many different styles of communication and here I focus on four broad styles that are widely used in personal relationships. These are passive, aggressive, passive-aggressive and assertive.

**Passive communicators** usually avoid direct communication. They tend to follow other people's ideas or allow others to make decisions for them, rather than sharing their own opinions, feelings, needs and desires. They put other people's needs before their own and find it challenging to say 'no'. They often avoid problems and conflict, and have 'people pleasing' behaviours.

The negative effects of people pleasing behaviour stem from thinking that others won't like you if you don't do what they want. This is based on a need to be loved, thereby creating insecurity and low self-esteem. To break this pattern, it is best to take small steps to express your needs and learn to say no to people in order to say yes to yourself. The more authentic you are, the more people will respect your decisions.

**Aggressive communicators** are direct about their opinions and tend to force their ideas onto others, often choosing to make decisions with a disregard for other people's feelings or needs. They use controlling behaviour which can come across as bullying and frequently push others away.

**Passive-aggressive communicators** combine both elements of the passive and aggressive styles. They tend to communicate in indirect and passive ways, often saying yes to things at the time, yet come across as sending confused signals and carrying feelings of guilt about their decisions later. They have difficulty expressing their thoughts, feelings and needs, repeatedly being dishonest with themselves and using control tactics to get their way.

**Assertive communicators** express their thoughts and feelings with respect whilst being in tune with their own and other people's needs. This helps to build healthy, balanced and respectful relationships. It's the most effective style of communicating as it creates openness, honesty and the courage to speak your mind.

It's possible to have a combination of communication styles, with most people tending to lean toward one particular style. It's all about being balanced. It reduces the risk of misunderstanding if you go with the flow yet communicating your feelings and desires in a direct way, whilst still maintaining connection.

Take some time to identify how you tend to communicate and understand how your style may be affecting your relationships. You can then work towards communicating more consciously and assertively with others. **What if you can become more assertive in your style of communication?**

## How do you communicate with others?

There are many modes of communication. Text, calls, talking, chatting, emails, touch or silence. What's your preferred way of communicating? Chatting can work if both people have that preference, but note that to make the right choice it's important to be aware of the other person's preference. If they prefer calling then use that method instead, as this will create a meaningful connection.

Technology has made it faster and easier to communicate about simple things, like letting someone know you are on your way home or posting pics. Just don't make it your main mode of communication, especially when you have something important to talk about. Nowadays, it's shocking to hear that there are people who even choose to break up with each other via technology as they feel safer. When you use technology to communicate, you should even consider how you are writing something. Have you ever received a text or email that is written in CAPITAL LETTERS? How did it make you feel? It can come across as being shouted at! This alone can trigger a negative response to the person receiving it.

If someone is being unresponsive by not calling or texting you back, ask yourself if this bothers you. Take some time to reflect in your journal and answer these questions:

- How does it make you feel?

- How can you change your attitude?

- What's the story you are telling yourself inside your head?

- What conclusions do you come to?

- What behaviours will make you more receptive to communication?

Consider that there may be other reasons for them not responding. Not everything is about you. Remember when you do next speak that the flow of the conversation will be smoother if you're in a good mood versus if you're feeling the effects of having had a tough day. Choose the right moment to prioritise your partner and schedule time to have a conversation. Ultimately it all comes down to teamwork and great communication in relationships. When you need to talk more, let your partner know. All it takes it a little more care and attention.

When communicating with someone who you want to have a relationship with, either through chat or text, make it interesting! Build on the conversation instead of responding with one-word answers, or pick a topic that you know the other person is interested in. It shows you have a genuine interest and can lead to you taking it to the next level.

**What are the different forms of communication?**

> 'Raise your words, not your voice. It is rain that grows flowers, not thunder.' – Rumi

There are three broad types of communication: non-verbal, verbal and written communication.

**Verbal communication amounts to only 7% of communication.** These are the words that are spoken.

**Non-verbal communication amounts to 55%** and is made up of our body language, physiology, and facial gestures. The figure 55% comes from research that Albert Mehrabian undertook in 1971, the results of which are still often quoted today. The remaining **38% is our tone & voice** (how we say the words).

**Communicating without saying a word**

Given that body language and facial gestures make the most impact, when you do not use words, you are actually saying much more at a subconscious level. Your silence can speak volumes. The interpretation of body language can be based on a single gesture. Smiling or hugging are powerful gestures of expressing yourself non-verbally to another. The other person will feel the love and care in your embrace. It may even encourage them to show care to another in a similar manner!

Did you know that just by observing someone's body language and their eye patterns over time, you can tell if they are being dishonest or truthful? Unfortunately, most people don't take the time to be attentive to the clues.

**Written communication**

There are many benefits to written communication. There is something special about writing a personal handwritten note or sending and receiving a card to a loved one. You get to touch and feel the person's message, which brings a sense of joy and re-connection; you feel loved and valued. Expressing yourself through a written letter can help to make you feel closer to the other person.

People who write a shopping list or a to-do list are more likely to stick to it and get more done. Plus, it sends a message to the brain that you have accomplished something! If you want to manifest your ideas and dreams into reality, writing down your thoughts and then vocalising them will accelerate the process.

Through an exercise like journaling, you can get the thoughts in your mind down on paper to obtain some clarity in your thinking. Not only does it release negativity or emotions, but it also starts the process of healing and breaking patterns. It may help you find something that you do need to communicate to establish trust and connection.

## Loving expression

**The words you speak and the vibrations you send have the power to deeply heal and comfort, not just your loved ones, but all people across the world.**

Loving expression is where you feel safe to be yourself when communicating. Unfortunately, as we grow up, we inherit obstacles to this relating to our family upbringing and circumstances. Maybe it wasn't accepted to express love openly, to say 'I love you' or display public affection. In some cultures, this is still a reality.

It's important to feel good when you communicate, to feel free to be yourself with respect for another and without the fear of judgement.

Sometimes you may not know how to verbalise what you are thinking or feeling, so you keep it inside you and repress these feelings. Ideally, you should **say what you mean with love** and make your feelings heard. If you don't, you may let out all your feelings without thinking about the impact this may have on the other and later regret it. **The quality of your love life is based on the quality of your communication.** If you want to improve your love life, it all starts with how you communicate firstly with yourself and then with others.

If you are upset about something, it's most likely based on the meaning you have associated to it. If you want to change your life, it's not the event that matters. It's what you do with the thoughts you have about it that determines the quality of your communication and life.

Almost all pain in your life starts with a feeling of loss. For example, if you have lost love, you feel you have a sense of loss or something is missing. However, you don't have to go looking for love; **you can't lose love that is already inside of you**. Following the feeling of loss, comes hurt and that leads to anger and later comes out as resentment and confrontation.

In any communication with another, the response you receive is either a loving one or a cry for help. It all comes down to how you choose to respond. If you respond back in the same way, it just won't work! To enhance your relationships, choose to communicate consciously by raising the quality and vibration of your choice of words, the tone you use to deliver them, your facial gestures and body language.

> **How do you feel communicating with loving expression could benefit your relationships?**

**It's time to fall in love with the truth of who you are and experience an authentically expressed life.**

One moment you are in love as things are going well. Yet as soon as something goes wrong, or isn't to your liking in the relationship, it turns to hate. It's the people you love the most that you show your true colours to. You believe they will just tolerate you for who you are or think they will always be there, even when you are behaving at your worst. The fear or insecurity of losing them or being abandoned may also come into play and cause you to react in a certain way. You become entangled in love. So many people end up taking their partners for granted or stop talking to their family members or friends due to misunderstandings or wanting to be right or in control. How can we so easily judge and pour negativity onto our loved ones when we later regret it?

When it comes to our professional life, when communicating with managers, or work colleagues, we have a lot more to risk in terms of our reputation, status and even losing our job and income. We somehow manage to bite our tongues, hold back and assess the situation carefully, taking the time to reflect and resolve issues or carry on tolerating things.

Take a moment to reflect in your journal and ask yourself, if you have judged others:

- What causes you to criticise and judge, especially loved ones?

- How does it serve you or them?

- What makes your character or personality change in these situations?

> **What if you could be more authentic in your words and actions in both your personal and professional life?**

## Power of responding

**When you can't control what's happening, challenge yourself to control the way you respond. That is where the power is.**

There are many external situations in our life that we cannot control – the weather, other people, government, etc. We may react negatively

159

to them or take things personally. This happens when we do not feel in control of the situation or aligned within ourselves.

Think of a time in your life when you have been upset or angry with your partner or another person. What led you to react or behave in that way? Next time, step into the other person's shoes before you react. It may be harder said than done! Have a think about where the other person is... what's going on for them in their life? **Remember, we can all choose how we respond in the moment.**

- How can you respond instead of reacting?

- How does it make you feel?

- How does it make them feel?

**"**

**What if you can consciously become aware of the way you respond? What if you could communicate from a place of love and compassion?**

**"**

---

### Exercise: *THINK before you speak*

Can you think of a time that you said something to someone and later wished you hadn't?

The point here is that your thoughts and words have tremendous power and transmit energy that cannot be taken back. Before speaking just pause, think and breathe. Here are 5 questions that can help you reflect and **THINK** before you speak:

T: Is it **True**? Is what you are saying based on fact or opinion?

H: Is it **Helpful**? Is it beneficial to the other person and relevant to their situation?

I: Is it **Inspiring**? Are they going to feel transformed by what you are saying?

> **N**: Is it **Necessary**? Is what you have to say really necessary? Can you let it go?
>
> **K**: Is it **Kind**? Is what you are saying showing kindness and bringing out the best?

Every thought emits a frequency towards the universe and that frequency returns towards the origin. So, if you have negative thoughts, you will in turn receive negativity. That's why it's so important to take care of the quality of your thoughts and words and learn to cultivate positive ones.

### What are the barriers to communication?

One of the main barriers to open communication is telling someone what to do. It can be irritating if done in a controlling way. No one likes to be told what to do. In fact, some may even go ahead and will do the exact opposite. Learning how to build rapport, influence and suggest ideas to the other person instead will allow more receptivity to talk further about an issue or an idea. Better still, take some time to brainstorm ideas together, with no limits.

### Why don't we communicate or spend time together anymore?

There are many reasons communication breaks down. Some of the main ones are not giving enough attention or affection to your partner or distracting yourself with digital technology. We become self-absorbed in our own needs and agendas. Quite often you may feel like avoiding your partner if you are not in the right mood; maybe you are stressed or don't have enough time. When your partner is feeling miserable and doesn't make an effort, you in turn don't feel like bothering about them. However, if the relationship is important to you, you will find a way to make it a priority and give it the time it deserves. Also take responsibility for your own happiness, rather than depending on the other person to make you happy.

## Setting healthy boundaries

We are all one and connected with everything and there should be no boundaries in love. After all, we are looking to bridge love. However, we may need to set healthy personal boundaries from time to time depending on the relationship and situation, especially if it feels toxic.

Personal boundaries serve as a guideline to communicate your physical, emotional and mental limits to another, to build a healthy relationship. It helps you to establish a safe space and consider what you can and won't accept. It is an act of self-care as you are putting yourself first. Some examples of this could include honouring your feelings, maintaining personal privacy and choosing how you share your space, time and energy with others. Be respectful of yourself and others. Work towards resolving any issues and reach out for some support if you need to. Make a list of some of your ideas to set healthy boundaries.

## Communicating about children

We may meet our partner when we are young and over time, we develop different interests and needs in the relationship, causing us to change and grow.

### Bridging boundaries

*I worked with a lady who got married at a young age. The couple had spoken about wanting children when they were first married. Although they had agreed a timeline in principle, her career took off and she had an opportunity to study and travel with work. Although, her husband supported her, he didn't communicate or express his true feelings as he didn't want to upset her. Instead he went along with it. Over time he became resentful of her success and new direction in life which created conflict in their relationship. I could see how using passive behaviour and not setting healthy boundaries had caused this miscommunication. I worked with them to understand their communication styles, align their values and release the guilt. They were able to have the courage to open up and support one another and came to a mutual agreement about balancing her career and starting a family.*

As a couple, it is really imperative that you keep communicating openly about your goals, dreams, passions and vision to support one another, otherwise you will end up drifting apart. There should not be any unnecessary pressure or expectations put on another to have a child. Instead consider all the factors carefully, including finances, as this may have a strain on the relationship. Adopt an attitude of patience, allowing space and time to process any thoughts and feelings and come to a mutual decision. Come up with a joint vision for your relationship that feels realistic and healthy for both of you and keep reviewing it in case of things changing.

On the other hand, it's totally okay if you decide consciously that you do not want to start a family or are experiencing fertility issues. Think about birthing in other ways. It doesn't necessarily have to be about a child. It could be using that creative energy to birth a new project, a business or possibly write a book or create some other dream you want to manifest.

**Building rapport**

People like people who are similar to them or who are similar to how they would like to be. Think of someone you like. What is it that you like about them? Maybe it's the sound of their voice or their style? Have you noticed when someone is responsive in a relationship, it's because you have something in common with them? Rapport is powerful when there is connection and spark in communication.

The best way to build rapport is by matching and mirroring. This method was created by Dr. Milton Ericson who was a medical doctor and hypnotherapist. He studied people and observed how they became like each other in a variety of ways, by the way they mirrored each other. You can build rapport by mirroring each other's body language (their posture, gestures, matching eye contact), their volume, tempo, tone of voice and the words they use. When communicating pay attention to your proximity to them by giving them their space and not getting too close for their comfort. Get into rhythm with their pace of breathing. When shaking hands or touching them you can match their style.

We build rapport with people in very natural ways. The stronger the communication between you, the easier it gets. To get a real experience of this you need to practice it consciously. For new relationships, or to enhance communication with someone you already know, practice matching and mirroring them for 10 minutes and notice the results. You will learn what works when you are in rapport and what doesn't work when rapport is broken. It will bring you closer together.

---

**Exercise: Communication works!**

Think of times in the past when communication and rapport were going well in your relationship. What specifically worked? Was it the time you took out to explain things or your emotional or mental state at that moment in time?

Remember the more you give of yourself authentically in a relationship, the better the relationship will be.

---

## Courageous conversations

*The quality of your relationship lies in the courageous conversations you are willing to have.*

The most important part of communication is the quality of your conversations and how much rapport is built. Communication issues arise when one or the other can't express themselves properly for fear of being criticised and judged. If this continues, it can turn into negative thinking. You may ask yourself 'What's the point?' and at that time a conscious choice is made to keep quiet. This further aggravates the situation and nothing gets resolved. Instead both people end up doing their own thing to keep the peace, or talking to someone else about their issues, and not having the courageous conversation for fear it will lead to another argument. Does this sound familiar?

If your partner complains that you're paying more attention to your phone or friends than your relationship, that's an issue you need to take seriously, even if you don't agree. The fastest solution is to sit down together and come to an agreement. There could be an agreement that you do not check email, social media or phone messages during specific times, such as on date night, at mealtimes, or when either of you needs to talk. It's important that this agreement feels fair to both of you so that you make the relationship work. When you do talk, there are two skills that are equally important – listening and asking quality questions.

These may sound like very simple skills. However, it's astonishing to see how many people don't do it right, as they've become accustomed to their natural habits and need to break free to form new ones.

So, what do you do if you do not get the response you want from your partner? You need to learn to be more flexible in your communication style. Either rephrase what you said or use a different perspective so that your partner understands you and receives it in a language they understand. These skills should be practiced so you get better over time.

**Listening with your eyes and heart**

Only hearing what you want to hear in a conversation, instead of listening for intent based on someone's life experiences can cause misinterpretation in relationships. Deeply listening with our eyes and heart can help build a soulful connection and open up communication.

*'So, if you will listen carefully,*
*Not only with your ears,*
*But with your eyes and with your heart,*
*Maybe somehow, we can communicate.' – Herbert G. Lingren*

# Deep listening

There is a reason why the Creator has given us two ears and one mouth. We need to practice deep listening twice as much. What kind of listener are you? Are you somebody who listens whilst waiting to speak? Do you only share your perceptive, not taking any notice of what the other is actually saying? Maybe you take over the conversation completely or try to fix their problem. Perhaps you are not that interested or drift off somewhere in your mind, leaving the other feeling ignored and frustrated.

Someone who listens well, learns. There is so much power in listening and giving your full attention to someone. When you are a good listener, it shows you are interested in what others have to say and curious to learn more about them. Interestingly, the word 'ear' sits right in the middle of the word 'heart' (h-ear-t). The ear is the way to the heart. So if you want someone's heart, learn to listen to them! Listening intently also allows you to better remember what the other person said. One of the best feelings you can have is when someone remembers what you said, whether it was a day, week, month or years ago.

As well as listening, you need to be mindful of the words and tone when communicating as it can change the entire meaning of what you're saying. This has an effect on your relationship and the attraction between you. There's also that dreaded phrase that people use, 'we need to talk', that conjures up thoughts of finding out something bad, when it could just be a conversation about vacation plans.

Listening helps to solve problems, resolve conflict, reduce stress and tension and build intimacy. When you feel listened to, it gives you a chance to gain clarity over whatever is bothering you and clear up any misunderstandings.

Practice to also listen to your inner voice before communicating. When you are truly deeply listening to another with all your being and presence, you become aligned with their feelings and can connect on a deeper level, possibly discovering something wonderful together.

**I am only responsible for what I say, not what you understand.**

It may sound simple, yet it surprises me how many of my clients get themselves into all sorts of distress by not listening or not being present or misinterpreting what is being said by another and giving it their own meaning.

If a man doesn't like the sound of something being said or the tone of a woman's voice, it is perceived as complaining, whining or nagging. This not only builds up frustration for both, but also causes disconnection.

I had a client who told me that her partner never listened to her. He would switch off mid conversation and she needed to keep asking him if he was still listening. In response she would get a 'hmmm' or 'yes' but in a tone that didn't satisfy her. She got frustrated internally and accused him of not caring about her, bringing up stuff from the past, unable to complete her sentences or get her point across. This ended up with him shutting down, unable to respond and walking away.

Whether you are a man or a woman, there will be times where you feel unheard or distracted. When both people recognise and question their own style and behaviours, and practice these key tools for communication, they can create a more conscious, harmonious relationship.

If you feel you don't understand something, it's best to ask for clarification and summarise the conversation. There is a difference between what a person's intention is and the words they've used to convey this versus what another person hears and perceives according to their model of the world. You should stay open and listen for the positive intent and deep meaning for the message behind the words.

Imagine you are watching your favourite programme and your partner decides to strike up a conversation. You are so engrossed in the programme that you tune out your partner. It's only when you shift your attention from the TV to them that you can really understand what they are saying. Men are often seen as culprits of this or they choose to become selectively deaf! There is a myth that women are good at multi-tasking but they get distracted too. They often miss the most important cues or misinterpret their partner.

**Avoid using the words always or never**

If someone ever has told you, 'You always do this and never do that' or 'you are never there for me', does it really make you want to listen? No. It feels like an exaggeration of the truth and can make you feel defensive. It is not an effective use of language and won't help you build a connection. There are other ways you can express your truth.

**Use 'when', 'what', 'how' statements.**

Instead of generalising with 'always' or 'never', get specific. Being specific will make the person feel like you are not judging their whole character, but rather looking at a specific behaviour. This can relate to either a positive or negative statement.

For example, yesterday (when something happened) when you left your clothes on the floor (what they did) it made me feel like you didn't notice or appreciate the effort I put into cleaning (how it made you feel). This sentence clearly tells your partner what makes you feel good instead of expecting them to guess.

Try to focus on the positive whenever possible. You and your partner want to make each other feel good, don't you? If you want your partner to help more around the house, focus on what your partner does, rather than what they don't do. Make them feel good about it by communicating your appreciation. You could say, last night (when) when you washed the dishes (what) I really appreciated it because I was tired (how you felt). Your partner will be more willing to do the things that please you if they feel a genuine recognition of what they've done and understand how it made you feel. Make a conscious decision here. What tends to happen in relationships is that people point out the negative more than the positive, which of course means they get more of the negative. It doesn't have to be that way.

**What colour is your heart today?**

We are asked how we are, or we ask this question to others, on a daily basis. Have you noticed most people are not even consciously aware of how they respond? For example, some respond by saying, 'I'm ok', 'I'm fine' or some even say, 'I'm not bad thanks'. In terms of this last one, did you know that the brain does not understand the word 'not' on a subconscious level, so you are supposedly saying 'I'm bad'! Something to think about it...

Become more aware of the response you receive as it will give you clues into how the other is really feeling. Better still, make the conversation more interesting by asking heartfelt questions. Some examples could be 'How have you been feeling today?', 'How can I support you?', 'Who or what has inspired you today?' or 'What are you looking forward to?' Keep it playful. You could even ask them, **'What colour is your heart today?'** This communicates that you care, dives deeper into getting to know the other and makes the conversation and relationship more interesting.

*What if you could listen for inspiration, joy, compassion and love? Practice listening to the sounds around you and the sound of your inner being? Do you like what you are hearing? Become an observer of the life that surrounds you.*

**Here are 6 simple tips to help you to become a better listener in your relationships:**

1.  Adopt a receptive mindset and have an attitude that is open and non-judgemental to your partner's perspectives. Drop your assumptions.

2.  Take time out to listen. Turn off any distractions and stay present by working on your mindfulness skills.

3.  Talk face to face. Avoid discussing serious issues in writing or via technology.

4.  Be curious and have a willingness to learn.

5.  Summarise and state what you are hearing. Your partner will appreciate you and it builds trust and connection.

6.  Listen to non-verbal clues (the words beneath the words) and connect to the emotion.

## The secret is asking quality questions

To make relationships work, we need to be aware of our own personal expectations, as well as those of the others involved. These need to be made clear to avoid misunderstandings. Asking powerful quality questions can help you to discover and become aware of what the real issues are and open you up to new perspectives. Learning to look at the relationship from the other person's eyes, allows you to connect with empathy before opening up to having a conversation.

Sometimes it can feel challenging to put ourselves in someone else's shoes if we may be going through our own stuff or have our own stubborn ways of thinking or holding onto some unhealthy emotions that we have not dealt with. The suggestion here is to clear these as much as you can so you are more available to yourself and to the other.

---

### Empowered to speak

*I worked with a woman who couldn't express herself to her husband. When she would approach him to talk about her problems, he would say that he was tired and that it was never the right time and got angry. She was going through a lot of change having moved to a new country and was reliant on her husband for support. She had become absent minded and lost her self-confidence. She felt anxious and had developed a cyst in her ovary. When we worked together, she uncovered a memory from her childhood where her father had become angry with her for forgetting to do something, after which she would either seek his approval before acting or avoid asking him. I could see that she wanted to express herself, to be listened to and was holding onto fear. I asked her what needs to be said that was never said. For the first time she was able to empty out, to speak from her heart. The tears just flowed as she released the pent-up emotions that were stuck in her throat. She was able to forgive her father and husband. I also spoke with her husband and he realised that it was more beneficial to ask her quality questions about how she felt instead of telling her what to do. She became more empowered, more confident to make her own decisions, started to heal and felt safe to speak. This brought them much closer to one another.*

---

### Do you ask open or closed questions?

**Open questions**: these start with 'how', 'what' or 'tell me more', such as 'How can I help you?' or 'What can we do?' They lead to open conversations and exploring possibilities that may not have been considered.

**Closed questions**: these result in a 'yes' or 'no' answer and sometimes can close the conversation down. If you need more information, closed questions are a great way to summarise and to get clarity on a specific point. i.e., 'What you are saying is............... right?'

Using a combination of both open and closed questions can help empower your communication in relationships.

**Here are some empowering questions to ask yourself:**

1. How would my relationship change if I improved my use of language?

2. How can I communicate more effectively so that I feel heard?

3. How does the relationship look when I look at it from the other person's eyes?

---

### Exercise: Listen for feelings

The first step is to address how it makes you feel when you are not being heard or can't express yourself. This will help you let go of any tension that has built up.

Take some time to just sit quietly and, instead of running away or distracting yourself, close your eyes and listen to your thoughts. Drop from your head into your heart.

How are you feeling? Where do you feel it in your body? Give it a number from 1 to 10, where 1 is no feeling and 10 is high. If it had a name what would it be called? Just allow yourself to be with the feeling.

You may also want to write down your experience in a journal or write a letter expressing all your concerns, feelings, etc. Make it as long as you like. Pour it all out onto paper.

---

**Make commitments to improve communication in the relationship.**

Take some time to create a list of ways that you and another can make a better team. Each of you should offer ideas to improve the relationship, rather than pointing out what the other person should do. Remember it's a team effort. If you feel like you have nothing to change, you're not being realistic. We can all improve in some area of our lives.

Commit to one or two small changes you will make each week. Encourage each other and recognise your efforts. Changing in-built patterns can take time, so commit weekly to new things you are willing to do or re-commit to old ones you still need to work on.

## LOVE model for communication

**Use the following acronym to help you remember some key steps for effective communication:**

**L – Language.** Listen and be mindful of your words

**O –** Be **Open** to observe without judgement

**V – Vulnerability.** Speak from the heart

**E – Express** your truth with ease, encouraging each other

As you will see, there's a lot more to communication that meets the eye. It's an art and takes practice and patience. Having an attitude of light-heartedness enriches your relationships and creates intimacy and connection.

# Chapter 8

# Connection Bridge

———— ✑ ————

*Love is not about forcing anything in your life, whether it is conversations, relationships, connection or attention.*

In this chapter, you will learn how to **connect for deeper meaning and purpose** within yourself and with others so that you **build intimacy and trust** and never have to feel lonely again.

## Transform conflict to connection

Connections are formed through the relationships you have with another, groups, yourself or a higher source. When there is a lack of connection, you feel disconnected and it can bring up many issues, fears and feelings of loneliness.

Coping mechanisms for a loss of connection may result in co-dependency, possibly staying in unhealthy relationships and doing whatever it takes to keep the connection safe. Some seek out a relationship as they have been feeling lonely. They adjust their needs, thoughts, feelings and interests and only show the parts of themselves that will satisfy the other. After getting that connection, they slowly reveal the suppressed parts of themselves to their partner, which changes the dynamics of the relationship. This then creates conflict.

Love has the power to heal and transform conflict. When you love someone, you have the tendency to want to offer them something and the desire to make them happy. The practice of mindfulness can connect you to love. It is just taking that moment to stop and become aware of yourself, your environment and the people around you. Mindfulness enables you to become present to what is and move you from conflict to connection.

**Desire for connection**

There are two basic forces within you that create conflict. One is the need for self-preservation, where you build walls around you leading to self-imprisonment. It keeps you safe and protected and is limited to your physical body. The other is the longing for freedom and connection. You want to expand your energy so that it feels limitless.

This creates inner conflict as we have many parts within us. The root cause of the conflict between these parts is whether your needs for connection were met as a child by the people that mattered the most to you, i.e. family and care givers.

---

### *Integrating desires to freedom*

*I worked with a woman who had a desire to be in a loving, romantic relationship (physical) and at the same time she longed for deeper connection, freedom and love with the divine (spiritual). She felt guilty for doing either. I could sense how she had separated out the two desires in her mind causing inner conflict. I guided her through a process of self-enquiry where she learned that the intention for both parts served the same purpose – obtaining connection. She was able to integrate a new-found love for herself within her heart. She discovered that she could fulfil both desires by creating balance, which brought her much joy and peace. She also obtained the freedom that comes through feeing aligned with purpose.*

---

There are many different levels of connection in relationships, be it psychological, physical, emotional, spiritual or at a communication level. Here are some examples: respecting each other's feelings, intimacy, appreciating unique personality characteristics, awareness of beliefs and values, communication styles and a shared meaning and vision for life.

Without a strong connection in place, it becomes challenging to have effective communication. There is a difference between being independent and doing your own thing, and being interdependent in your relationships. This is where you work together, creating balance and supporting one another whilst maintaining your own personal growth.

A healthy relationship requires different aspects of connection for it to last. While physical attraction, passion and sex is important, it is equally vital to connect from the heart. When the initial excitement and physical attraction and chemistry wears off, there would be an issue if there's not also a heartfelt connection in the relationship. Ensure you build connections that you value; appreciate the relationship, have the other person's best interest at heart and share moments where you lose track of time together, such as having meaningful conversations and showing genuine care.

Using substances to create connection are a sign of an unhealthy addiction. It may give you a rush of confidence to connect in the moment but, once it wears off, it can have a negative impact on your self-esteem.

**Connection, compatibility & chemistry**

Connection and compatibility are two different things. You can be compatible with someone, working well on something together and learning to build connection, yet not necessarily agree or like everything they do. Have you met people who are in love, yet not compatible, and stay together as they have a strong connection? Compatibility can be based on certain traits that you like in another, such as their interests or background. Some people even use astrology signs to see if there is some level of fit. It can work when there is a true connection to start with and there is a desire to take some interest in the other and appreciate the differences. The more compatible you are in terms of core values, the easier it will become to navigate relationship challenges.

You can build chemistry and yet it might fizzle out over time. Whereas, if you have a strong connection, even if you haven't heard from someone in a long time, you can pick up where you left off. It's best to work on building your connection.

It may take some courage in the beginning to connect with someone, especially if you are single and looking to find your ideal mate, but anything is possible when you go about things in the right way.

**You cannot force a connection**

We meet the right people at the right time under the right circumstances when our vibrations match. What really gives a relationship meaning beyond compatibility and chemistry is when someone connects to you with an understanding of your needs and treats you the way you want to be treated. They are committed to investing in you. This requires nurturing and can only happen if you also are willing to treat yourself and others with love, respect and are aligned with your values.

You cannot make someone love you by doing more for them. Attraction and love are created when you are just happy being you, doing your best to become a better version of yourself. Sometimes it can be as simple as giving yourself and the other some space to create desire by appreciating who you both are.

## What is emotional connection?

Emotional connection requires the most sensitivity of any of our needs, so is the most essential to practice. A strong bond is created through deep feelings for one another. It is important that you connect and care about each other's feelings if you are to engage in a meaningful relationship. The connection grows stronger between two people when they are interacting together physically in person which creates intimacy.

Take a moment to reflect in your journal and think of a time you had a pleasurable, intimate experience or a deep connection with someone. Take yourself back to the thoughts, feelings and sounds you heard at that time. How was that experience for you? When you focus on these moments, it can take you back into a feeling of joy and love, as you are connecting with yourself emotionally.

> **What if you could connect with yourself and come into oneness?**

It is said that men are more visual and logical in their approach to relationships. It takes them more time to open up and build a deeper connection emotionally. If you want to feel more connected to another, then being non-judgemental and respecting each other's needs will help create a strong bond.

When you do not want to engage sexually and are not feeling very connected to the other, turn your attention to your emotional state and do what it takes to bring that into your heart and communicate your truth.

**Here are a few ideas to get you emotionally connected:**

The eyes are the windows to the soul and communicate your emotions. The eyes can never lie as feelings reside deep within you. It's hard to hide behind them as you emote from your eyes. Have you noticed that people can be saying all the right things about being happy or having it all together, yet they may have sadness in their eyes? Having observed many people, before and after working with them, it was clear to see their emotional state had shifted once they had let go of any heavy emotions. They had regained that 'sparkle' in their eyes.

---

**Daily Practice: Connecting through the eyes**

When you are speaking to your partner or another, look into their eyes. Also listen with your eyes. Give the person your complete attention. Practice this regularly and notice where the other person is emotionally. With practice you will be able to tune into their feelings. They will feel your love and connect at a soul level.

---

*'When you love someone, the best thing you can offer is your presence. How can you love if you are not there?' – Thich Nhat Hanh*

---

### Connecting in presence

On my travels, I connect with strangers wherever I go. Whilst sitting on a park bench in Moscow, a Russian girl came and sat down next to me. Back then, I couldn't speak a word of Russian, yet I could see from her eyes that she was deeply distressed. I turned my attention to her and gestured if she was okay. A few seconds later, she bubbled up into tears. As I sat with her, I connected to her energetically by becoming present, maintaining eye contact and offered her comfort with a tissue. I held the space, surrounding her with love as she released her emotions. She gave me a hug afterwards, and her eyes looked brighter as she smiled.

---

Emotions are a universal wordless language. It reminds me of a statement made by Maya Angelou that 'people will forget what you said, people will forget what you did, but people will never forget how you made them feel'. This quote is still relevant today and signifies the importance of always leaving people better than you found them. Sometimes all the other person needs is for you to be there – a hand to hold, an ear to listen and a heart to understand them. Offering your presence can work wonders.

*When there is love in any given moment, there is an element of flow and ease, energy and allowing grace to work through you.*

## Building intimate connection

Intimacy is one of the most wonderful things there is about being human. Think of intimacy as Into-me-I-see. Intimacy starts with seeing into yourself first. The more inner connection you have, the better you know and love yourself, the happier and younger you can become. It opens the door to an even deeper connection when you're sharing that intimacy with someone you love romantically, from a place of building trust.

## Strong relationships are built on trust

When you trust someone, you feel comfortable confiding your truth and feelings with them. You feel they have your best interests at heart. We place our trust in the hands of others, whether it is with strangers, friends, family, colleagues or a partner and often this trust can be broken due to our expectations of the other. Not trusting others deprives you of human connection and makes it difficult to live to your full potential. Love is about trusting yourself to recognise your own strengths. Learn to be kind by spending the needed time to connect with yourself or others who you know are consistently there in your life to help. If you want trust, are you also being trusting and offering that in your relationships? It works both ways. In order to earn trust, we must learn to trust ourselves fully.

If you are in a relationship, your partner will not be able to be everything for you or fulfil your every need for love and connection. Likewise, you will not be able to fulfil the same for them. Instead of becoming disappointed, stay open to building new connections. Different people can offer us different perspectives and ways to feel connected and loved.

During my time in India, I spent time with people from different walks of life in ashrams and spiritual communities. I sought out environments which were conducive to my growth, sharing space, eating, and deepening my connection to myself with a greater purpose and mission of serving others. Through these experiences, I learned the process of getting out of my own way, seeing good in everyone, being grateful and learning to forgive those who have betrayed my trust. Investing in your personal development, with good teachers, can help you find purpose and connection in life. When our relationships feel strong, trust can feel easy.

When people are new to relationships, intimacy is important. It's essential to let it develop organically instead of rushing into things.

Intimacy is about feeling safe to open up with yourself first, so that you can open with another, lowering any defences that you may have. It could be just a smile, touch on the arm or even having the courage to look into the other person's eyes for a little bit longer. It takes time to build this sacred connection and feel this level of comfort but with practice it will begin to feel natural. An opening of the heart takes place, feeling safe to trust as you allow another to enter into your sacred space through mutual respect and patience.

This deepening and opening in connection then blossoms in every aspect of your relationship. It creates the kind of love that is just as passionate after many years together as it was in the beginning, and often even more so.

### Sacred space

I worked with a woman who had been married five years and was experiencing intimacy issues with her partner. Although she adored him in every way, when it came to physical intimacy her body just shut down. She was unable to feel deeply connected with him. It had taken her a while to adapt to her new way of married life. There was also a lot of expectation from her family to make the marriage work. She had a longing to start her own family and felt guilty that she could not open up fully to her partner. Together we created a safe space for her to uncover her issues and got to the root cause which was linked to sexual abuse in her childhood. She started the process of healing, building a bridge of love and connection with herself. She was able to fully let go of the pressure and experience a deeper physical intimacy with her husband from a safe and sacred space.

Intimacy comes from a place of non-judgement for yourself or the person you are with. It is about the willingness to be vulnerable, to be there for yourself unconditionally and allow others to do the same without putting up any barriers. It's about honouring them to become aware of what they require. Intimacy is often what seems to be missing or fades away, especially in longer-term relationships.

Intimate connection is not just sexual. Loving and caring for your partner with non-sexual touch generates oxytocin in both men and women. At the physical level, there is a desire to fulfil a sexual connection, to be adored and be touched with affection through being intimate. Holding hands, using loving words, hugging and smiling are all considered small acts of intimacy, ensuring your partner feel wanted. Time, space, patience and preparation are needed to build intimate connection.

**5-minute exercise to building intimate connection**

This exercise is best done with your partner. However, it can also be practiced with a friend or on your own.

**Exercise: Energy of the heart**

Get into pairs. Decide which partner is A and which is B.

Sit facing one another. Place one hand over your partner's heart and your partner places their hand over your heart.

Now take a moment to close your eyes and just feel into the energy of their heart. Partner A: Share what you notice about your partner's breathing.

After a while you may notice that your breathing becomes synchronised.

Now switch to Partner B.

If you are single, you can do this by placing your hand over your own heart, close your eyes, notice the breath going in and out and follow the rhythm of your heartbeat. Notice how you feel emotionally and mentally.

## Power of hugging

Hugging is a powerful form of connection. The average length of a hug between two people is three seconds, but researchers have discovered that when a hug lasts 20 seconds it has a therapeutic effect on the body and mind. The reason for this is that a sincere embrace produces a hormone called 'oxytocin', also known as the love hormone, lowering both our heart rates and cortisol levels. Hugging also helps to increase our self-esteem, to prevent disease and makes us feel a lot happier and calmer.

We feel comfort every time we have a person in our arms, whether this is when we cradle a child, cherish a dog or a cat, when we are dancing with our partner, or simply holding the shoulders of a friend. You might think it's just a simple hug and take it for granted, yet in reality it is much more than what it appears. It's the purest gift of love you can offer to another. It's a moment of deep connection, created through becoming linked with another's soul, filled with affection and bliss.

---

### Daily Practice: Hugging prescription for happiness

Your prescription for the next 21 days is to give your partner a hug each day. This could be first thing in the morning, when you come home from work or before you go to bed. Make the hug last at least 20 seconds. Make it a routine every day and watch what happens. Your relationship will become sweet like honey.

If you are not in an intimate relationship, find someone to hug everyday. It could be a family member, close friend, colleague or your pet. Give yourself a hug everyday too.

---

*Psychotherapist, Virginia Satir, said, 'We need 4 hugs a day for survival. We need 8 hugs a day for maintenance. We need 12 hugs a day for growth.' Whether those exact numbers have been scientifically proven remains to be seen, but there is a great deal of scientific evidence related to the importance of hugs and physical contact.*

## Connecting to your values in love

Your values develop subconsciously over time from childhood. These get formed from your environment, life experiences, family, friends and society. To really know yourself and connect to the heart of another, it is key to discover what is important to both of you. Unfortunately, many people rarely understand the other's values and outlook on life, or their own.

Awareness of values helps you to discover the impact they have on everything else in your life. Our values influence our thoughts, which impact our feelings, the decisions we make, our behaviours and actions, which then become our results.

You may need to ask yourself some powerful questions before even figuring out what your values are. What is truly important to you, your priorities and why? If you don't know what is important or are not self-aware, you will probably make the wrong choices in your life. Values help you to measure the progress you make in your personal growth and development. If we look at connection as an example... take a moment to consider what it means to you. Why is it important? What does connection give you?

What qualities do you possess? Here I am not talking about what you do or what you look like. Your values are at the very core of your being. They're what you truly stand for, your strengths, your enthusiasm for life and growth, what gives you happiness. They're what make you unique. It's more about your character, your beliefs and who you are becoming. Letting go of any judgements will help you to start being more accepting and kinder to yourself. There is always a kinder way, a more compassionate reaction you can have with others and yourself too.

If someone disrespects your values, you can often feel this in your body. When this happens, some choose not to address the issue. For example, if one of your values is integrity or honesty, and then you find out that someone has been lying or hiding something from you, it can leave you questioning yourself and the relationship. Choose to value yourself and demonstrate your standards, especially if you are just dating. The earlier you do this, the better. Don't just morph into someone else's values because you want them to like you.

If your partner is always too busy to spend time with you, and you seem to be the one giving and prioritising your time around their schedule and needs, it can eventually make you feel resentful or angry. When they do spend time with you, then you may feel great. However, when they get busy again, you may start becoming needy and being more generous, i.e. cooking their favourite foods just to get their attention. Instead, learn how to be more inter-dependant and focus on what's important to you. They then won't be responsible for taking care of your needs. It allows freedom and growth on both sides. It reminds me of one of my favourite sayings by Jim Rohn:

*'The greatest gift you can give someone is your personal development. I used to say, "if you take care of me, I will take care of you". Now I say, "I will take care of me for you, so you take care of you for me"'.*

When you are really into someone, you just want to make them happy and do as much as possible for them. It can get really intense or feel controlling. You think that just because you love someone, they will love you back. If you love them through your generous, supportive ways, they will see your value and you will become indispensable. Notice when you feel desperate for connection or try to hold on to someone, your focus tends to move away from yourself, by doing more, giving your time, gifts, and doing what they want to support them.

### Exercise: Discover your values

Discovering your core values will help you to understand yourself and others better, enhancing connection and communication in your relationships. Below I've given some examples of common values that are important in a relationship. This is not an extensive list as there are literally hundreds of them!

Think about the values that are important to you in a relationship. From the list below, choose and write down every core value that resonates with you. Do not overthink it. As you read through, simply write down the words that feel like a core value to you personally and what it means to you. Please feel free to write down values you possess that are not on the list.

Appreciation, Acceptance, Adventure, Balance, Compassion, Connection, Contribution, Energy, Family, Fun, Flexibility, Freedom, Gratitude, Growth, Harmony, Happiness, Humour, Health, Integrity, Joy, Kindness, Love, Making a Difference, Openness, Passion, Peace, Quality Time, Respect, Service, Security, Team work, Trust, Understanding, Wealth.

*Look at the values you've written down. List all the ones that resonate. Group them in a way that makes sense to you. Now pick 6 that you intuitively feel are closest to your heart, ones you couldn't function without, and prioritise the list. These are your core values.*

*Now that you have discovered what they are, ask yourself:*

- *What did you learn about yourself?*

- *How is your life in alignment with these values?*

- *Does your current relationship meet all these values?*

---

### Mismatch of values

*I met a couple who were very much in love with one another. However, they couldn't understand why they seemed to disagree when it came to spending time together. The husband loved to play golf and do outdoor activities, whilst his wife enjoyed being at home, reading, cooking and spending quality time with herself or her partner. Having coached them about what was important to them, it became apparent that they had some conflicting values. The husband had adventure as one of his top values and his wife had security. Once they realised the differences, they were able to work through their issues and start to appreciate and support one another better, giving each other time and space to appreciate what was important to them.*

## Demonstrate your values

The best way to demonstrate your values is through your communication and engagement in your relationships. It can help you become more decisive and focused on your outcome. Start becoming lighter in your conversations by perhaps adding some humour. It shouldn't be serious every time you speak, otherwise it can leave you feeling like you are responsible for fire-fighting each other's problems. You could become aware of your surroundings when you are out and start noticing what you are doing consciously. To make the conversation engaging, share something you both feel passionate about. Have you noticed you light up when connecting about something close to your heart? When you feel lighter you are more fun to be around and it keeps the connection alive between you.

When you are able to have fun doing what you love, either on your own or with your friends, it strengthens that inner connection. Do you know that you also become more attractive to another when they see you in your flow, doing what is important to you? This creates the space for desire and leads to an increase in intimacy and passion. There is nothing more wonderful than seeing your partner happy doing what they love.

One of the most important values in relationships is balance. Without the right balance, you're left feeling off centre and disillusioned. If you are overplaying your values by being too giving, appreciative, nice, kind or not being truthful, honest or realistic, you will be out of balance.

Having observed and spoken to many couples, it's fascinating to watch how they demonstrate their values through connection, showing affection and supporting one another.

*'Let love be the spaces in your togetherness.' – Kahil Gibran*

*The love of togetherness*

*I met Margaret and John in a store when they came to purchase an outfit for a special occasion. They had been married for almost 40 years. I could see they had a glint of love and joy in their eyes, as if they had just met. It was adorable to see them holding hands. John valued Margaret's input when it came to shopping for clothes. She knew exactly what suited him from style, colour, size and comfort. They had mutual respect and honesty between them and a playful way of teasing each other.*

*Whilst John was trying on his outfit, I got into conversation with Margaret and asked her what the secret was to love and happiness in their marriage. She told me they were best friends. In fact, they had only argued three times in the whole of their 40 years together! Not a bad word was said between them and they never went to bed angry. She shared how they spoke about everything openly, and made uninterrupted quality time for each other, whether shopping, eating or just going for walks. She told me, most importantly of all, they had a deep understanding of what the other valued. Their focus was on making each other happy. When John came out, having overheard our conversation, he smiled and added that most of all they still treated each other just as they did when they first met. Nothing much had changed, just a few grey hairs, and they'd grown to be more in love. They were such a beautiful couple and their story is truly inspirational.*

## Bring 'spark' and passion into your relationships

The spark between two people comes from being inspired to tap into your creative force and re-invent yourself and the relationship. In India, some couples told me they felt compromised due to the stereotypical roles in a relationship. Typically, the role of the man was to go out to work, whilst the women stayed home and took care of the family. Their relationship became routine and boring, more like a friendship than a romantic relationship. They lost meaningful connection and intimacy over time. Things are fast changing where more couples are making efforts to re-invent themselves, connecting openly about their needs and values and co-creating a life together so that both feel happy.

When was the last time you flirted with your partner? It's wonderful if you can treat them like a lover instead of taking them for granted. Simply being a bit more flirtatious, complimentary or showing some playfulness can re-kindle that spark of passion between you.

Sex for a woman starts hours before – stroke her desire, give her compliments, discover what turns her on. Men are drawn visually to women and are attracted on a physical level. There's a joke I heard that goes something like this: men are visual and women are more auditory, that's the reason why women wear make-up and men don't listen!

When it comes to having sexual intimacy, it should not feel like another task. In fact, some of the most loving couples schedule uninterrupted quality time together, creating the right ambience. Breathing in unison and coming into rhythm with your partner when you make love creates oneness, instant intimacy and connection. Experiment and explore together using different tools and techniques to find what works best for one another.

If you want to bring that passion back in a relationship, try going back to how things were when you first met. What did you love doing together? Re-invent yourself regularly and create a sense of curiosity to keep the spark alive. Discover new things about the other. Create new memories by doing creative things together; make it exciting, take some risks and respect your differences. Take it in turns to do what makes each of you happy. Be adventurous and go on surprise dates. Take time to compliment your partner or write them love notes. Keep checking in with each other and most of all re-visit your values and vision together to keep you on track and keep growing.

**Wired for love**

Seeing another person's perspective and where they are coming from is more important than just focusing on gender expectations. Paying attention to the little things can make a big difference in your relationships and keep things in balance. Little things done consistently over time provide extraordinary results in the quality of your relationships. For example, women may often feel hurt and rejected if their partner does not show them affection in a particular way. For a woman it could be receiving more hugs and compliments. For a man, he needs to feel in charge and often women can push men away if they are too demanding. Your use of language could be used to help you to connect better i.e. saying that something makes sense or is a good idea!

Relationships can be enhanced when we learn how we are wired in the brain. Men and women are wired a specific way for love. Men tend to be more attuned to the left side of the brain, which is more analytical, adept at problem solving and more likely to take a logical approach. Women are naturally attuned to the right side of the brain which is more connected to their feelings, intuition, creativity and nurturing qualities.

When you enter a new relationship or you go somewhere new and different, it stimulates a chemical in the brain called dopamine. Dopamine gives us focus, motivation, passion and happiness in our relationships. When you are wired for love it makes you feel high. However, when your hormones become unbalanced it can cause stress. High testosterone levels in males helps keep men's stress levels down. On the other hand, low testosterone levels can cause depression.

With an increasing number of successful women in the workplace and a pressure to perform, the stress can sometimes create more testosterone (the male hormone) within women.

---

### *Balancing energies*

*This reminds me of a story of a couple I worked with. The man had previously been the sole provider in the home and lost his job. Although he did his best to find work, he was unsuccessful. His wife, previously a housewife started to work and became the provider. There was a shift in the dynamics of the relationship. He started to physically withdraw from her as he didn't feel good enough. His wife couldn't understand as she was doing her best to provide for them and thought this meant that he was having an affair. They were on the brink of a divorce. All that had happened was that the wife's energy had become more masculine in nature; as happens in so many women, they become the providers and feel the need to do everything. Their roles had switched. We worked through the issues and they came to an understanding of this and, over time, they were able to reconnect and regain intimacy.*

## Masculine and feminine: energies for connection

Whether you identify as male or female in your body, everyone has both 'yin' (feminine) and 'yang' (masculine) energies within them. You are not created to be equal but to balance yourself and each other out, just like a battery has both a negative and positive charge to function. In nature, the Sun is masculine whilst the Moon is feminine. If you are a woman, think about how the Moon aligns to your monthly cycles.

Feminine energy is currently rising on our planet. Here I am not talking about woman empowerment; women are already empowered as they have the ability to give birth. Women know the important qualities of nurturing, loving and protecting, as do men. I'm instead referring to the fact that, in the past, feminine energy was suppressed or devalued in society and masculine energy was more valued and celebrated. You are an expression of the divine and need to celebrate both parts.

As the energies and times are rapidly changing on the planet, the shift in how your feminine shows up is seen in how you communicate and connect. A man still needs to have a mission, purpose and work that provides fulfilment for his happiness. He isn't looking for a woman to fulfil him. He wants to provide something for his partner that makes him feel worthy. However, men cannot progress if they do not let feminine energy in.

Many of my male clients have also had too much feminine energy. It's okay to be sensitive and show your emotions as a man, but when a man is just pleasing the women in his life and not in touch with his masculine side, he ends up being treated poorly.

### Mr. Nice Guy

*In the case of one client, who obeyed his mother's every need after his father's death and later got married, he turned into 'Mr. Nice Guy'. He was unable to truly express himself for fear of upsetting his mother and women around him and allowed them to dictate his decisions and push him around. Deep down he felt resentful, as he wasn't getting his needs met. We worked together to understand his patterns and help rebalance his energies so that he was able to tap into his masculine energy and feel more powerful and in control of his decisions.*

**Guided process to balance your feminine and masculine energies**

Sit comfortably and find a quiet place. Close your eyes and scan your body and notice where you have any physical pain, tension or tightness.

Notice if this feeling is on the left side, where feminine resides, or the right side, where masculine resides.

Imagine the part of you in that area and see both sides standing and facing each other. Listen to what it is telling you it needs. Imagine the other side of the body hearing that need and acknowledging it. Go ahead and have a conversation and listen to the response. Once it feels complete, let them slowly walk together and meet each other in the centre of the heart. Imagine them embracing and hugging each other, with the inner male and female coming together in harmony and becoming one to receive, honour, connect and serve each other. Give thanks and say 'and so it is'. Now open your eyes and write down any insights from this process.

**The root cause of loneliness is not feeling joy, connection and love.**

### *Hungry for connection*

*Rita, one of my seminar participants, would sit in front of the TV on her own when everyone had gone to bed. She would get her secret stash of chocolates out of the cupboard and before long would consume most of the box whilst mindlessly watching TV. It led to her feeling bloated and concerned as this was turning into a daily unhealthy habit and causing weight gain. When we worked together she told me she missed her partner who had left her. I could see how she was using chocolate to comfort her need for love and connection.*

*Food is one of the most common go-to things as it satisfies all needs. After just 20 minutes of working together, she realised that the emotion at the root cause of her behaviour was loneliness and released it. She has since completely stopped eating chocolate and become healthier and happier with new-found ways to connect to herself and others.*

**If you have ever experienced loneliness, what did you do to overcome it?**

**What resources do you currently have in your life to help you meet and connect with people who are aligned to your values?**

Remember, we may come into a relationship with past hurts, unmet needs, and parts of us that need growth. When we let go of these defences and open our hearts to each other in a relationship, we create an opportunity for both of us to heal and grow, as we journey together through life.

Some people do not feel enough within themselves. They want to include something else as part of themselves. Love is a longing to include a part of yourself. If this longing finds a physical expression it becomes sex, if it finds a mental expression it becomes greed, if it is emotional we call it love.

**Conditional love** is selfish and ego centred. It only lasts whilst certain unspoken rules and conditions are met by the other. Examples include:

'I will only love you if you do what I say or if you make me feel good about myself.' It has conditions attached to it and is transactional. Gradually, unspoken rules come into place that neither of you agreed.

**Unconditional love** is where you love others exactly as they are without imposing any desires, rules or expectations on them. You feel completely free, limitless and selfless. An example of this is, 'I love you no matter what you are, think, feel, have, believe or do. I love you simply for being you and I give you the power to love yourself'. There are many ways to say I love you. You just have to listen out for them. Someone could ask you if you've eaten or ask you to call when you get home. These are subtle loving messages.

The voices in your head come from your ego type. They create feelings of resentment, blame, jealousy, separation and being a victim. When we learn to bring our awareness from our heads to our heart voice, we come to an understanding on unity, gratefulness and happiness, and move from being a victim to being a victor.

Love is a vehicle for oneness. Love can be experienced by spiritual practices including meditation, yoga (meaning union) and prayer. This brings you into completion and oneness with all of you.

## What is detachment?

**Detachment does not mean that you should own anything. It is more the case of nothing should own you.**

You cannot truly detach from anything as we are all connected. We are all one. If you are detaching because you feel that person or situation will go away, you are mistaken. The thought of detachment comes up when we feel afraid of getting involved, or not wanting to be hurt by another. Detachment is a way of avoiding life.

On the other hand, getting attached to someone can also bring a fear of involvement or commitment; you don't want to be hurt or rejected or hurt the other, you sometimes don't fully accept or receive the love from your partner or you feel out of control.

For some involvement is thinking you will get entangled with another and experience pain and suffering, whilst attachment is being identified with things that you are not. To become attached is to live in fear that what you want will not materialise and traps you in a continuous state of unhealthy desires and patterns of co-dependency.

> **What if you could become detached from the thoughts that hold you back and instead become involved with another from a space of freedom and love?**

**How can you know life without becoming involved?**

Quite simply, without involvement there is no depth of experience in your life. People need connection and purpose to survive in the world. It could be through music, art, helping others, or bringing children into the world. Whatever you choose, be involved fully in life and do it from a place of childlike wonderment and joy, with an open heart.

---

### Letting go of baggage

Another perspective to the art of detachment is to live a minimalistic life, to detach from material, declutter and only use what you require. Travelling around India with no home base, limited storage space and having weight restrictions on internal flights allowed me to practice these detachment principles. It really is surprising how much you don't need, and it taught me to stop hoarding things. Have you ever bought stuff that you didn't really need? All this does is bring more stress, debt, and overwhelm. Is it really that important to hold on to baggage just for the sake of it? I experienced the best feeling when giving things away and seeing the happiness it brought to people who were more in need.

---

Many times, we may carry baggage from past relationships, which stops us from attracting the right relationship or causes issues in our existing relationships.

When you let go of things or people you don't need, you will feel abundant and light, open to manifesting new experiences into your life and feel a sense of joy and freedom.

**Energetic cord cutting**

When we connect energetically to another, individual cords or energy tubes of either love or fear are formed. They consist of particles of energy that originate from our energy centres that connect with people, ideas, situations, places and ideas. As we connect to them, we either draw energy or we project energy onto others. When there is an unhealthy, imbalanced or toxic relationship, there is a high chance of becoming attached by unhealthy cords which can keep pulling our energies. These unhealthy cords could be created due to fears that arise based on survival instincts, low confidence, unhealthy behaviours, co-dependency and addictions. Even though you may be doing everything right in your life, things may not feel right because you are still connected energetically and feel stuck, unable to move forward until you cut the cords and heal. If these cords of past connections are not cut, over a period of years they drain you of your energy. Cutting the cords in an unhealthy relationship will lead to detachment, setting both parties free.

You have good energy cords too that extend from your heart to someone you love. You cannot cut these cords. You can enhance and expand these cords just by thinking of someone and projecting energy from your heart to them, showering them with love and affection.

Many women have shared how they developed gynaecological issues resulting from being in unhealthy and toxic relationships. These conditions usually develop in the second chakra, the sacral centre; this is the connection to our emotional body, sexual organs, fertility and creativity. It's essential to consciously clear up any pent-up emotions and heal any sexual ties so that you feel balanced and grounded to Mother Earth and connected with your body. Visualising the colour orange and sending light to these body parts is deeply healing.

Cord cutting can assist if you are trying to move on from someone, especially in romantic relationships. Setting them free in this way is the deepest and purest form of love. You can also use it for day to day challenges, such as a toxic environment, person or situation.

When doing the process, it's important to remember that you are not detaching from the love. This love is always here. You are detaching from the behaviour and negative energy.

There are various methods to cord cutting. I have guided many clients, adjusting the method according to their specific situation.

---

### Cutting cords with love and connection

*I worked with a young man from Mumbai who had lost his father when he was a baby. He was left to care for his mother and siblings as a young boy and this caused a lot of anger, frustration and stress as he felt like he was carrying a heavy burden of responsibility. Although he loved his family, he saw his life as a struggle, and felt blocked in his career and purpose. During our session, we discovered that the root cause of his issues was connected to losing his father. He was finally able to let go of all the pent-up anger and grief and come to forgiveness with his father, releasing the burden of responsibility, and cutting all the unhealthy energetic cords from both parents. All that remained was gratitude, love and a deeper understanding and connection to self which left him feeling happier, lighter and hopeful to create his new future.*

---

## Connection through love languages

We looked at love languages in the second chapter of this book and here we will explore them in more detail. As a quick reminder, there are 5 ways to express love: physical touch, quality time, receiving gifts, acts of service or using words of affirmation.

The client story below demonstrates how you can turn around a relationship in times of stress by paying a little attention to your partner's preferred language to rekindle love and connection and become present to their needs.

### Don't touch me!

When my client Valerie got stressed, she actually disliked physical touch, which happened to be her partner's love language, as it made her feel unloved. Valerie's preferred love language were words of affirmation, which is exactly what stressed her partner out! Her husband hated being verbally reassured when stressed and would rather Valerie just be quiet and give him a cuddle. Valerie was so happy to learn this because her first instinct would have been to start talking! Her husband quickly learned to reassure Valerie in times of stress using words of affirmation, appreciation and recognition instead of physical touch. The love and connection between them grew with this new-found understanding of how to use their love languages to connect in good and bad times.

Becoming more aware of your preferred language and putting it into practice will improve connection between you. While it is great to be aware of the love languages as a tool for a healthy relationship, they should only be used in a conscious way. Use them as a way to show love to one another, not as a reason for being upset with one another. The greatest love languages include compassion, patience and being present.

Here are some ideas on how to use love languages in a healthy way. You can also create your own.

1. Send an unexpected note and encourage your partner genuinely.

2. Use positive criticism and reward the efforts not just the results.

3. Be enthusiast when it comes to gifts. Remember special occasions and make it a priority to send thoughtful gifts which enhance personal connection.

4. Plan a quality hour; eliminate distractions, become present and create time together for focused conversations and activities.

5. Create daily magic moments, possibly walks, watching the sunset or sunrise. It doesn't need to be a big holiday!

6. Serve each other; share chores, make breakfast or dinner and do the dishes together.

---

**Exercise: Discover your love language**

Now have a think about which is your preferred love language. What resonates with you? In times of stress notice where you seek comfort to feel connection.

---

**Daily Practice: LOVE Connection Model**

Use the following **LOVE acronym** to help you remember how to connect with others on a daily basis:

L – **Look**        – use eye to eye contact

O – **Openness** – be open in mind, body and heart

V – **Values**      – become aware of what is important to you

E – **Empathy**  – be compassionate to where the other person is coming from

---

Connections that are based on true love are those that come from the heart of who you are. You feel a sense of genuine care and interest in the other and are being your authentic self in how you show up.

# Chapter 9

# Self-Love Bridge

———— ✐ ————

*'Love is the energy for life, and everything is energy.'*

In this chapter, you will learn how to tap into your **energy body** to **love** and **care for yourself** through **acceptance** and **forgiveness**, so that you experience more **compassion** and **gratitude** and **become loving** in your relationships.

## The language and vibration of love

When you learn to become mindful of the energy behind your words, thoughts and actions, you can use this as a powerful tool to create a loving vibration within yourself and in your relationships. This understanding happens within the heart, creating a spaciousness and oneness within, which transforms you into love. It's based on a sense of presence and pure conscious awareness of your being in each moment. Every part of our being speaks a different energetic language; the language of the physical body is energy and frequency, for the mind it is words and images and for the emotions it is feelings.

Be mindful that you speak to yourself in your head more than with anyone else, therefore choose to be kind. This self-awareness allows you to have the power to choose to engage in the language and vibration of love in all your interactions.

Whilst we may find ourselves getting easily upset when someone says something unkind to us, we also feel healed and soothed when someone says something kind and loving to us. This energy works in both ways.

> **What if you could focus your energies towards being more kind and loving to yourself and others?**

### Raise your love vibration

To keep your vibration at the highest level, focus on the vibration of love and unity consciousness which is a lot stronger than the vibration of separation and victimisation. When you send that energy out, others resonate with this frequency creating harmony.

We are beings that vibrate at certain frequencies. Each vibration is equivalent to a feeling and in the 'vibrational' world, there are only two types of vibrations, the positive and the negative.

Love is a vibrational frequency that flows from the heart towards the mind to help purify and free it from suffering and pain so that you can experience true freedom. On a practical level, we can engage with the mind and emotions to create what we desire. However, we also have a personal energetic field and frequency that helps us to attract what we want. Given how the **Law of Attraction works**, you magnetically draw things to you vibrating on the same frequency. This means that if you work to maintain a high frequency (through love, peace and joy) then you will naturally manifest more good things in your life.

Having directly experienced working with energy through practising and teaching Tai Chi, Qi Gong, Reiki and emotional freedom healing, I started applying these energy practices into my own life and with my clients. I noticed energy levels shifted from feeling low, frustrated or scattered to that of peace, love, joy and creating abundance in all areas of life.

So how does this vibrational scale work? Well, imagine a scale of 1 to 1,000 where 1000 is the highest state of consciousness you can attain as a human being. At this level you would be an Enlightened master, i.e. Buddha, God, Christ consciousness.

The vibrational scale is a tool for measuring personal energy, which was introduced by Dr. David Hawkins in 2002. According to Dr. Hawkins, when you are at a vibrational energy of 500, you can lift 750,000 people around you. When someone hits 700, they positively impact 70 million people!

As illustrated below, at the lowest level of the scale is where there are heavy emotions such as unworthiness, sadness, guilt and shame. These vibrate at lower frequencies causing suffering and an inability to thrive, as we've accumulated energy blocks and negative conditioning throughout our lives which cause pain. Feelings like love, bliss and enlightenment vibrate at higher, uplifting frequencies. **The vibration for love** sits somewhere **between 500Hz and 540Hz. Without love there is no joy.** Therefore, to get the best out of life, we need to raise our energy vibration to feel more joy and love. This happens when we clear our energy blocks and have the courage to take inspiraction, which helps us to come into acceptance, harmony and balance.

| Vibrational Emotional Scale | |
|---|---|
| 1000 | God Consciousness |
| 900 | Gratitude |
| 780 | Appreciation |
| 700 | Enlightenment |
| 600 | Peace |
| 540 | Joy |
| 500 | LOVE |
| 400 | Reason |
| 350 | Acceptance |
| 310 | Willingness |
| 250 | Neutrality |
| 200 | Courage |
| 175 | Pride |
| 150 | Anger |
| 125 | Desire |
| 100 | Fear |
| 75 | Grief |
| 50 | Apathy |
| 30 | Guilt |
| 20 | Shame |
| 0 | Death |

Expanded

Contracted

Your vibrational frequency can be affected and measured by a number of factors including your immediate surroundings – your home and environment, the people you surround yourself with, the conversations you engage in, the colour of the clothes you wear and even the amount of money you have in your bank account and the quality of your lifestyle.

Whether at home or at work, if you spend much of your time in a disorganised and unhealthy environment, this will affect your vibrational frequency. Overcome this by organising yourself and keeping your environment clean. Show the universe that you are willing to create space to receive much more and be thankful for what you already have.

The people around you directly influence your vibrational frequency. Surrounding yourself with the vibration of complaining, indecisive and pessimistic people will decrease your frequency, affect your wellbeing and prevent you from attracting and manifesting into your life that which you desire. Therefore, choose to surround yourself with happy, optimistic, loving people to enter into a similar vibration.

---

### Change your frequency

A client of mine previously watched movies and listened to music that spoke of betrayal, sadness, heart break and abandonment. I asked her to pay attention and notice how it made her feel. She quickly realised the impact this was having on her moods and love life. She is now much more aware of what she feeds her mind, has changed her playlist to one including more loving and happy lyrics and engages in inspirational movies and conversations that uplift her. Just by changing her frequency she became much happier within and attracted a wonderful relationship into her life.

---

All energy matter vibrates at different frequencies. Higher frequencies impact what you attract and lower frequencies keep you stuck. The key is to clean up your thoughts and raise your love vibration. The energy of the heart and love is a frequency that is on the rise, as many more people are spiritually attuned, which will shift vibrational reality and influence change in the world for the coming decades.

**Exercise: Frequency of love**

Now think back to a time when you either met your partner or someone special who gives their love and support to others unconditionally.

- What was your state of mind and the vibration you were emanating?

- What were your energy levels like?

- What were you thinking about and saying to yourself?

- Where were you on the vibrational scale?

What is it about them and their energy that lights you up?

Think of how they make you feel when you are with them. Imagine being surrounded with this frequency of love and it becoming a new way of being.

When clients come to me wanting to attract new relationships, the first place we start is to identify their current vibration and work towards raising their love frequency. You rarely manifest anything new in your life from a low vibrational frequency. The art is to keep your vibration at a high peak as you work towards what you want in your life. In the following daily practice are some ways you can do this.

**Daily Practice: 3 step process to raise your love frequency**

1. Give yourself some love; make some time each day to acknowledge yourself. Ask yourself, in this moment what is the most loving thing I can do for myself? And then go do that! It could be making yourself a cup of tea or having a power nap.

2. Acknowledge love every day in your life, whether it is the love for your parents, siblings, friends, co-workers, pets,

neighbours or your partner. Be grateful for the love that you already have in your life. Often, we don't realise how much love we are surrounded by and take others for granted.

3.  Start practicing random acts of love in the world; it may a kind word, a compliment, a smile, a hug, or a kind gesture. Start to become an observer of love and notice what shifts in your life.

---

### Raise your vibration for more love, fun and joy

Cynthia was quite shy, lacked confidence and hardly went out on her own. She was desperate to find love, have fun and joy in her life. She had become isolated. By following the 3 simple steps to raise her love frequency, she became more aware of love in her life. She practiced random acts of love for herself and others, ventured out more, visited new places on her own, treated herself to whatever she needed in the moment and was generous with her time and energy. Her self-confidence levels increased and she became more attractive from the inside out. People started noticing her. She followed her passion and joined a book club, made new friends and started dating again.

---

The feeling of love and being in love is a frequency that you can tune into. Where do you feel it? Inside your body, mind or heart? Take the time to find your own frequency of love for your life, with people, experiences and yourself. Begin to live from that place and feel in love more of the time. You will experience a shift in your reality, the way you see others and how people treat you. Let that love come out to play!

### The sun of love is always shining

There are some people who have love inside them. Their presence just brightens your world. They have an internal being that transmits light and warmth, feeling like the sun on your cool face. It's a beautiful and calming energy which emits an inner peace, without wanting anything in return. It's about shining their love and light like the sun.

> **What if you could be like the sun, loving everyone?**

**Your energy speaks even before you do.**

First impressions are formed on your energy alone. Before you even start speaking, you've projected your energy out onto others. Have you noticed that you can have an instant connection or attraction with someone based on their energy alone? Have you felt that you just gravitate towards someone's energy? On the other hand, being on a higher frequency or wavelength from someone may mean that no matter what you are saying, they are unable to hear you or receive that message. It all has to do with our journey of growth.

This reminds me of the saying, 'you cannot talk butterfly language with caterpillar people'. In the birth process of a butterfly we have 4 stages – 1) the larva 2) the cocoon, 3) the caterpillar and 4) the butterfly. This simply means that there is a process of learning and development from under-developed, to developing into fully developed.

The language that is used to describe an idea must match the understanding of the person to whom the idea is being addressed. Hence it is a good idea to become aware of how you are putting your energy out as it reflects who you are and what you attract into your life.

Let's now take a look at how energy plays an important part in your body's system and how it impacts your emotions for love.

## Energies for love

*'A relationship begins with the meeting of two unique energies. Although invisible, the energy you and your partner bring to the relationship determines the way you communicate, love, fight and want to be loved.' – Donna Eden*

## What is energy?

Energy comes from various sources – the sun, air, and the earth. Apart from the energy we receive from food, air, and water, we also need other subtler energies. Various names are given to this energy such as Cosmic Energy, Chi (Ki) (Qi)Prana and Universal Life Force. The difference between someone who is alive and someone who is dead, is their energy. Energy is all around us and within us, permeating all of creation, keeping our bodies alive and healthy. Just think about electricity; you don't necessarily know how it works but you know it is there. It's energy – you push a switch, electricity flows through and the light turns on. You trust it works.

Emotions are energy in motion. Emotion is the experience of energy moving through the body. The Latin derivative for the word emotion, 'emotere', means energy in motion. These are sensations in the body, felt either through contraction when there is tension or expansion. To become aware of your emotions, you need to become aware of vital energy within the system which is communicated through your feelings.

## Energy medicine for self-care

**Self-care is giving the world the best of you, instead of what's left of you.**

Most people think that they don't have time for self-care as they've become so wrapped up in the busyness of their lives, striving to accomplish more or make ends meet. Yet self-care isn't just about pampering yourself by having a massage or taking a hot bath or shower. Yes, those things can help you to wind down, but it's so much more than that. Self-care can happen whilst you are in the flow of life, and can be done whilst working, meeting a deadline, having a conversation or cooking a meal. When you become aware of yourself, taking a moment to pause and notice your breath, checking in with your body and mind, you become present to your needs. You are worthy of your own love.

Self-care is when you tap into your energy, coming into a loving space, feeling the wonder of life and showing up with real kindness and care for yourself and others.

Energy medicine is the new medicine today. Instead of taking a tablet to relieve your pain, there are alternative, complimentary ways to learn how to enhance your energy for self-care and come into self-love.

I feel grateful to have learnt some energy medicine tools with a beautiful couple some 20 years ago in Turkey, who were personally trained by Donna Eden, the founder of this work.

*At the time my immune system had become very weak as I was recovering from Tuberculosis in my lungs. As I practised the energy tools, together with healthy nutrition, my body became much stronger and resilient and I was able to regain my energy levels and heal my body in very little time. I still practice these exercises as part of a daily self-care practice.*

There are times when many of us can give too much of ourselves and our energy to others, leaving us with nothing left for ourselves. You may have heard that expression, 'You can't pour from an empty cup. You need to take care of yourself first.' Every part of you is sacred. Self-care is about investing in yourself to open up to renewal, recovery and rest.

*My first experience of energy healing and self-care was after losing my mother when I learnt Reiki. Reiki is made up of 2 parts – 'Rei' meaning 'universal life or spirit' and 'Ki' meaning 'energy' or 'force'. Reiki is a form of alternative energy medicine developed in Japan by Dr. Mikao Usui in the early 1900s. Applying Reiki helped to balance my body's energy system (the 7 Chakras) and heal my heart. I have used Reiki with many clients to help them feel deeply relaxed, calm the mind and relieve stress and tension.*

**Exercise: Energy awareness**

Although we can't see energy, one way to become aware of its presence is through your hands, which have minor chakras that act as portals for energy, healing and creativity.

- Rub the palms of your hands together for a few seconds.

- Feel the heat building up in the centre.

- Now bring your hands, palms facing each other, in front of your body and start to become aware of the energy between your hands.

- Bring your palms closer or further apart (about hip distance). Feel your way into it. You may begin to notice a tingling sensation or some resistance or pressure between the palms. That's energy!

You may want to close your eyes so that you can feel this ball of energy and imagine it expanding. Then place this energy on your body, to an area that needs some loving care.

## The gift of love from childhood

*'Behind you, all your memories, before you, all your dreams, around you, all who love you and within you all you need.'* – Lilli Vaihere

The quote above reminds me how we can learn about love from children. Whether you have children or not, you have the gift of innocence and love within you from childhood. Children have boundless amounts of energy and love to give. They are hungry to learn and their minds are like sponges, soaking up as much as possible. They run around care-free and use their imagination to dream and play freely. As we get older, we forget this gift of dreaming and using our energy to create what we want. Children remind us how to connect to our own creativity and play with a childlike innocence and sense of wonderment, curiosity and fun and bring us into a state of presence, opening our hearts to joy and love. It helps us to remember that we start as love and return to love as wholeness.

> **When was the last time you allowed yourself to dream, play and create new memories?**

## The freedom of forgiveness

*'Forgiveness opens up a pathway to a new place of peace where you can persist despite what has happened to you.' – Les Brown*

Forgiveness is all about freedom. Please keep in mind that forgiveness is not for others; it is for you. It frees up your power, heals your body, mind, spirit and life. You don't have to wait for forgiveness to happen to you. You can empower yourself to take charge and open up to wonderful opportunities in your life.

It's easier said than done, and can be challenging to forgive especially if there is a lot of resistance, you felt hurt or betrayed by the other, or if you had chosen to carry out a specific role that may have involved some level of karma in the relationship. In each moment, we are given a choice. We can either look at our circumstances and be victims of them, or see them as a gift and a learning opportunity whilst understanding the part we had to play. Once we choose to forgive, we can break free of our limitations and come into awareness of reality and the power that lies within us. Do not allow the pain of the past to keep you from living in the present. Life is precious and can be short lived. Consider if you only had a week left to live; what would you choose to do? Would you focus on what is bothering you, how others behaved or complain about the little things that irritate and stress you? We can choose to suffer or choose to feel grateful. Who would you call and say sorry to? Who do you need to forgive?

### You are not your behaviour

There are people who may behave and act out in ways that you cannot comprehend at the time; perhaps they've used violence or have

209

committed crimes against another. You may automatically associate their behaviour to who they are. Yet beneath the behaviour is usually a cry for attention, to be loved and seen. Forgiving someone doesn't mean you accept their behaviour or trust them. It means you forgive them for yourself so that you don't hold on to negative thoughts and can move on with your life. Doing the inner healing work to come to an understanding of this can really help.

## Lessons from forgiveness

I realised that my father's behaviour in the past had nothing to do with who he was as a person. He had his own deep-rooted issues, which led him to act out in a certain way. Through releasing my emotions and reframing the story that I had told myself, I was able to transform my perspective and projections and come to a different interpretation of the truth.

*What I learned through forgiveness with my parents is that they are also God's children and did the best they could with the resources they had at the time. Their challenging relationship was an experience they had to go through to learn their own lessons. I just happened to choose to be born to them, and be a witness in their journey. The more I saw life through their model of the world, the more things started to make sense. They have given me a life-line to become the person I am today. I am eternally grateful for this profound gift of insight, for their love and blessings and for the courage and inspiration to grow. I wish them both peace.*

## How long does it take to come to forgiveness?

In the area of romantic relationships, some of my clients have come to me and asked how long it takes to 'get over' a relationship or deal with the hurt and betrayal so they can come to forgiveness. There is no time limit on forgiveness. It will vary depending on your conditioning, belief system and the willingness to break free of the negativity and unhealthy emotions that are holding you back. It takes both your personality or ego self and your soul's readiness to forgive. It can be a gradual process depending on how deep the hurt is. Forgiveness happens when it comes from a place of genuine willingness and you surrender to it. Once you can step into the other person's shoes, their mindset and feelings, you can empathise with them. Just like you, they want to feel love and connection. When you forgive yourself and others with an open heart, it gives you a sense of love, strength and peace inside. You are not only coming to terms with the past, but also creating your future. It is after all a journey.

## Ho'oponopono Prayer

One of the most powerful ways that I have learned to come to forgiveness and self-love is an ancient Hawaiian healing prayer called **Ho'oponopono.** The word 'ho'o' means cause, while 'ponopono' is perfection and translates to 'correct a mistake' or 'make it right'. It was developed by Kahuna Simeona and later experienced by a psychologist Dr. Ihaleakala Hew Len, who helped heal an entire ward of mentally ill criminals without ever seeing any of them. This spiritual prayer is simple to practice. It is important to open your mind to the understanding that what is in your life is 100% your responsibility. That's when your relationships will change for the better. This works through releasing any negative thoughts, memories or feelings that may have become blocked in your energy field. You just repeat these 4 statements either in your head or out loud:

**I love you**
**I'm sorry**
**Please forgive me**
**Thank you**

Once you see the story for what it is, and release it with respect, love and gratitude, the healing is complete. There are many deeper benefits to this practice as it also heals your ancestors and the karma that may have been built up over different generations and lifetimes.

## Karmic lessons

You may have heard the saying, 'What goes around, comes around'. This is what karma is in a nutshell. Karma, whether good or bad, is brought to you based on all of your actions.

Here we'll take a look at fear and love-based karma. Fear based karma is where your bad actions in the past negatively impact your current life, whereas love based karma is a gift that can bring you lessons for your soul's personal growth, and will continue to bring these lessons back around until you have learned them. Therefore, if you focus on hurt you will continue to suffer. If you focus on love, you will continue to grow.

## The art of apologising

If you feel you have hurt or offended someone through your behaviour or actions, whether or not you intended to at that time, it would serve you to acknowledge, apologise and repair the connection. Firstly, take ownership, no matter how uncomfortable it may feel. Just saying 'I'm sorry' is usually not enough, as it comes across as half-hearted. The quicker you can apologise, the better, rather than ignoring or defending your actions, or allowing things to brew up and get out of control. Resolve any misunderstandings and re-instate the relationship. This will also help you clear any karma. The best apology is changed behaviour.

## 3 step process for apologising

1. Say 'I'm sorry'

2. Clarify what you did (take ownership)

3. State what you'll do to correct it

Also learn to accept that you may not get an apology from someone who hurt you. Instead deal with your feelings, release them and thank the person for giving you the strength to grow.

---

### Exercise: Forgiveness letters

A cathartic way to release pain and hurt is to write a letter to the person who you need to forgive, expressing all your feelings and thoughts about them and the issue. Even though you may feel you don't want to re-build the relationship at the time, it will be a deeply healing experience for you and them.

---

1. Write down all the things that you may not have had the courage to tell them face to face. You will be surprised just how much may be buried deep within until you get it out on paper. It helps you to come to an understanding of what happened and brings to the surface any negative thoughts and emotions so that you can start to release them slowly and come to peace within.

2. Write down what you forgive them for. *I forgive you for* ....................

3. Keep going until you feel completely empty.

4. Acknowledge everything you need to forgive yourself for and your role in the situation. Write down *Please forgive me for* ............... Keep going. You can also read the letters out loud and record yourself so that you can be an observer and learn the lessons.

5. Now write another letter. This time express all the good qualities of the person and the lessons learned. Then ask for forgiveness. Put out a prayer that they too may find forgiveness for you in their heart and forgiveness for themselves.

6. Once you have written the letters, you can burn them. This sends out a prayer or intention that this issue be taken care of by source or God and any attachments be dissolved with love so you are both set free.

**"**

**What have you learned from forgiveness?**

**"**

# The heart to bridge compassion

## What is compassion?

> 'Compassion is a relationship between equals. Only when we know our own darkness well can we be present with the darkness of others. Compassion becomes real when we recognise our shared humanity.' – Pema Chodren

Buddha has defined compassion as love plus meditation. It is when your love is not just a desire or need for the other or asking for something in return. Instead you are ready only to give for the sheer joy of giving. When you add meditation to it, it becomes compassion.

Compassion is being able to appreciate and accept the emotional state of another person or yourself. It is not about suffering with the other, rather seeing life from the eyes of the other so you empathise with where they are and what they are going through. You are not there to fix them. It's about having a level of emotional intelligence that enables you to connect from your heart. All you can do is offer your love and ease their suffering. When you truly understood the pain beneath the behaviour, you discover a love that is so great, and yet unexpressed.

The best way to learn compassion is to come into acceptance of everyone and everything as it is. Let go of any judgement, expectation and the need to compare yourself to others and instead lovingly embrace your fears and imperfections. Compassion allows you to ignite the experience of love within you. This then allows love to flow from your heart as you express compassion to all those you meet and becomes the basis for how you interact in the world.

What you see in another exists in you at some level. As I mentioned in an earlier chapter, the idea that you project onto another is your perception. The compassion you have for yourself is mirrored in others and you experience that in return. Compassion is the key to bridging the love gap.

---

**Exercise: Compassion**

Take some time to answer the following questions in your journal:

- When was the last time someone showed compassion towards you? What did they do and how did it make you feel?

- Now imagine what it would feel like if you showed others some compassion. What might that look like or feel like for you? How would it change your life?

- When was the last time you felt compassion towards yourself? This is often one of the hardest things to do, and yet once we integrate this, it will bring endless joy.

Compassion is a quality that needs to be practiced regularly and built over time. It then naturally becomes part of who you are.

---

# The attraction of gratitude

'The miracle of gratitude is that it shifts your perception to such an extent that it changes the world you see.' – Dr. Robert Holden

### What is gratitude?

Gratitude positively affects your vibrational frequency. It helps to keep you connected in your close relationships as you appreciate the people in your life and their best qualities, remembering why you got together. The more grateful you are, the more attractive you will become. Gratitude is about having a great attitude to what has happened, what is happening and what is going to happen.

Incorporate gratitude as a daily habit into your life, starting right now. Thank and appreciate everything, from the good to those that you consider not good. Thank all the experiences and lessons that you have lived. Gratitude opens the doors for good things to flow and manifests positively in your life.

## Awareness of gratitude

Sometimes gratitude comes late. You initially may not appreciate or notice the little things that someone has done for you; you've instead taken them for granted. It is in the absence of someone in your life that you may realise what they meant to you. *What if you could express your gratitude to someone every day?*

---

### Daily Practice: Cultivate an attitude of gratitude

If you develop an attitude of gratitude you immediately go into a different vibrational frequency, which helps you attract more of what you are grateful for into your life. Even in your darkest hours, always find something to be thankful for.

From the moment you wake up in the morning to going to bed, feel grateful that you are alive and have another day to make a difference. A daily practice you can do is to bless everyone you meet and everything you have in your life, even if it's small.

Take some time to look around and notice what is here in the moment. What are you grateful for in your life? It could be as simple as your breath, your senses, the environment you are in, nature, your friends and family. Practice having good wishes for others. Blessings are so powerful and can transform people and situations. This creates good thoughts that become the experience and quality of your life.

Keep a gratitude journal and use it each morning and evening, listing at least 10 things that you are grateful for. Start with the statement 'I am grateful for...' or start with 'I am so blessed now that [a person/situation, etc.] has been resolved.' Remember to include all the areas of your life including health, relationships, career, wealth, family, development and spirituality.

---

---

**Exercise: Gratitude letter**

Now write a list of 10 things that you love about your partner or someone close to you. Write them a thankyou letter of all the things you appreciate about them. Describe their qualities that have had an impact on your life, such as courage, support, or kindness. How did it support you on your journey to who you have become? Then make time to sit down with that person and read your heart-felt description. Thank them for being an influence in your life and notice your relationship blossoming.

---

**Gratitude process:**

Over the next 7 days:

- Write down 3 things that you are grateful for in yourself

- Write down 3 things that you are grateful for in your relationship (if you are not in one currently, and want to be in one imagine you are)

  You will have built up 42 objects of gratitude that can help build love in your relationship.

## Loving self

*'Love yourself first and everything else falls into place. You really have to love yourself to get anything done in this world.' – Lucille Ball*

The path to self-love is an ongoing commitment of learning, re-birthing and strengthening the love within yourself at every stage of the journey. Some people think that when you say you love yourself it's being selfish. It's not about being selfish; it's an act of being selfless. It's the most generous gift of connection and love you can give yourself. You may have been conditioned to put others before yourself or have been burnt-out from loving everyone else, and it's only when this has consequences on your health that you realise the value of self-love.

217

You can't pour from an empty cup; you need to fill yourself up and take care of your needs if you are to be of true service to others. Take responsibility for your own happiness and life. Start to fill your cup with love so that it overflows. This way you come into an authentic space of abundance to give to others, which feels easy and joyful and happens naturally, without expectations.

Loving yourself is the recognition that you are already complete and whole, regardless of your relationship status. When you take care of yourself, you show up for yourself and others feeling empowered and approach the world in a different way. You are more present and able to contribute more of your energy, talents, love and self to another. Loving self helps you connect with yourself, your creativity and truth. It all starts from within.

Remember that love is who you truly are. Self-love is about tapping into the infinite flow of love, power and wisdom that exists within. You can spend a long time looking externally to that which is forever changing, yet fail to recognise that what you seek lies as a constant within you. One day everything just clicks, and you realise what is important to you and what isn't. You learn to care less about what others think about you and more about what you think of yourself. You remember how far you have travelled, remembering the times when you thought things were so difficult and dark that you would never recover. And you smile. You smile because you are truly proud of yourself and the person you've fought to become. You remember that you are love.

## Who are you becoming?

*Maybe the journey isn't so much about becoming anything. Maybe it's about un-becoming everything that isn't really you so you can be who you were meant to be in the first place.*

Hopefully, you have gone through all the chapters and applied the practices, processes and exercises. In this section, we will now take a look at how you can start to create your new identity and discover who you are becoming in love. This is less about doing, and more about being.

## Creating a new identity

Your identity includes many different aspects including your personality, looks, qualities, expressions, and beliefs, and how you may have moulded yourself to please others. Our identities evolve over time. We live in a world where we perceive ourselves through the perception of what others think about us and our true identity becomes blurred. I have seen this in companies where there is a requirement to adopt their values and expectations in order to be successful and rewarded. Relationships and life experiences teach you to grow and, without consciously realising it, your identity changes many times over. In the continuous journey of change, it can sometimes leave you questioning **who you are.**

*I had lost a sense of my real self at each stage of life, from losing my mother, getting married and divorced, entering and leaving relationships and leaving my corporate job. In order to follow my passion and dreams of travelling and running my own business, I went through a continuous process of re-evaluating what was important to me, letting go of the old and re-birthing my new identity and self. What started off as one month in India in an ashram village, extended to 7 years on a spiritual journey that allowed me to undergo a process of unlearning and becoming an observer of life. Layer by layer, I let go of all that I thought I was, all that I thought I had to be and, in that moment of pure awareness, realised that I am no one and no-thing; who I thought I was fell away. I was left without any identities or labels, as I remembered I am that I am. I finally came home to my true self.*

However, currently for us to live in this physical world and function within it, we need to re-create an identity for other people to make sense of who we are, our role and our work in the world. It also helps give us clarity and direction, keep us aligned with our values, and drives our vision, mission and purpose.

Your identity is a true reflection of who you are once you have quietened the inner voices and outer opinions and expectations of others, allowing you to come into full acceptance and love for all that you are. If your identity is that of someone who thinks they are not confident, that's what will become true for you.

---

### Creating a new future

I worked with a young, gay man. Although his parents were aware that he was gay and had a boyfriend, he still felt awkward around them. He was finding it difficult to fully express himself and move forward in his life. When he came to me, his energy was low. He told me he felt anxious about not being able to find a job and wasn't confident about offering financial and emotional support to his boyfriend. I could see how his mindset had created a lack of confidence and abundance, not allowing him to reach his full potential. Through our coaching sessions, he discovered that one of his values was freedom and although he enjoyed living with his parents, he was not expressing himself authentically. I asked him to step into times where he felt fully free and his physiology started to change. He became more energetic as he recalled those happy memories. I then asked him what he needed to believe about himself to feel confident and free. He answered, 'I am confident', 'I can do anything I put my mind to', 'I am proud of my relationship and am abundant'. This created a shift in his identity and helped him create a new future. He was able to attract a new job and move in with his boyfriend, honouring his value of freedom.

---

## How to build self-confidence

Self-confidence is about showing up as a full expression of who you are. Become aware and accept where you are. You can learn to build the muscle of confidence when you are willing to come out of your comfort zone by working on things that challenge you. Get comfortable doing things which feel a little uncomfortable. Without some level of challenge there is no room for growth. Ask for help and copy the role models who have already done what you aspire to do. For example, if you want to be more confident talking to strangers, start taking small steps by approaching people every day and saying hello to them. Then build it up to more people. Over time, you will start to feel confident enough to have a conversation beyond the small stuff and get comfortable to open up, learn more and change your life. Then practice, practice and practice some more on a daily basis! It takes time, dedication and consistency to build up your confidence. Remember Rome wasn't built in a day. It's a gradual process. Having a clear plan and sticking to it will help you get better results. Be compassionate with yourself and celebrate each milestone.

> **What commitment will you make to yourself to improve your confidence?**

**Learning to love yourself in relationship by creating your identity**

If you love someone else more than yourself, you will always compromise too much, ignoring the red flags, getting hurt and losing yourself in the process. You just can't love in a healthy way unless you learn to love yourself first.

Sometimes, when we get into a relationship, we forget about our needs. We may even start to put our needs on hold for our partner, family and friends. We could disconnect with who we truly are and what is important to us. When two people come together in a relationship, it's so important that they have their own identities instead of merging. The whole reason we're attracted to another person in the first place is their uniqueness.

Some people come together in the hope that the other person will help them find themselves. Some relationships help us do just that, if we are with the right person; they may not necessarily be the one that we had been dreaming about and who satisfies all our needs, yet they push our buttons or gently encourage our growth to help guide us to look within and find the parts of ourselves that need healing.

**Exercise: Creating your identity**

Review your relationship to see where you have things in common and hobbies that you have of your own. (It's very enriching when the two come together!)

Start creating your unique identity. Take a moment to reflect in your journal and think about the following questions, also adding your own ideas for re-inventing yourself.

1. What is important to you?

2. What do you want to achieve and why is it important?

3. What do you need to believe about yourself to have the life of your dreams?

Make yourself a priority and learn to say 'no' to others so that you can say 'yes' to yourself. Schedule the time needed to create the new you. Visualise it and feel like it has already happened. Keep thinking about it and focusing on it.

## How do you love yourself?

*'Never go in search of love, go in search of life and it will find you the love you seek.' – Atticus*

Love is our highest teacher, yet we can only spread love when we are in love ourselves, or when we 'are' love. We often look for someone to fall in love with, but the first person we need to be in love with is ourselves.

Love will offer you peace, and gives you the self-confidence to live life from your heart and connect to the source of life. Love will pour out of every cell of your being and radiate onto others. You will become a magnet for love.

To love yourself, dig within. Ask yourself quality questions that allow you to go through a process of discovery and healing. Start to accept yourself as you are, looking in the mirror and welcoming your soul; see God within you.

Of course, you'll have good and bad experiences. It's during those bad times that you need to embrace yourself even closer. What if there was nobody coming to rescue you? What if you could rescue yourself?

Can you remember who you were before you got into a relationship? What did you love doing? Some relationships totally transform us to becoming better versions of ourselves, whilst others stunt our growth and make us shrink. Learn to know the difference. Listen to your intuition. Learn to love without expectations.

> **How can you show some love to yourself today?**

**Exercise: Who are you becoming in love?**

What is unique about you? Where's your passion, your fire, your spark? It's your true character that wins in the long term. Let your personality shine through, be unstoppable and feel free to be yourself.

Take a moment to reflect in your journal. Who are you becoming for yourself, your partner (or future partner) to create the relationship of your dreams?

## Love all, serve all

**When we can learn to love all and serve all, relationships then become a true blessing instead of a power struggle.**

Once you have discovered who you are, connecting to your **spiritual body** and using your passion to be of **service** to others becomes your **purpose**. Perhaps your **purpose** right now is to be present with the people you love. Maybe your purpose later on is to learn something new. There are so many purposes in your life. It could be as simple as to help, to love, to learn, to grow, to enjoy, to celebrate, to contribute or to have a life that's meaningful.

Transitioning from your own growth to contributing to others enables you to be of service. Service is wonderful for your mind, body and soul, whether it's through your time, energy, skills, talent, money or loving another. You can contribute your time to something that is meaningful. You can give your energy and presence to others. You can offer your skills as an energy exchange. You can invest in yourself or sponsor someone else to make their dreams a possibility. You can become involved in a charitable cause, or help humanity alleviate suffering in the world. When you fall in love with yourself, you will become more available to love and serve all of life, allowing the divine to work through you.

### Learning about self-love from Mother Nature and the elements

Remember you are more than just this physical body. You are a spiritual being having a physical experience. When you notice yourself feeling out of balance and struggling with life, practice tuning into Mother Nature's cycles. The different seasons and elements will help you feel rejuvenated. Spring is when our intentions and seeds get planted, summer is the time for them to flower or turn into fruits, autumn teaches us about change and how to let go and winter is a time for silence, rest and reflection. Nature can teach us a lot about ourselves. Practice taking a moment to pause and look up at the sky. Embrace the vastness. Watch the sunset to remind yourself to be grateful for the day and welcome the sunrise as a new beginning.

| | |
|---|---|
| Remember you are **water** | – you are made to cry to cleanse, flow and let go. |
| Remember you are **fire** | – you burn, tame, adapt, ignite and create a spark. |
| Remember you are **air** | – you observe, breathe, focus and decide. |

| Remember you are **earth** | – | you are grounded, giving, you build and heal. |
| Remember that you are **spirit** | – | you connect, listen, have an inner knowing and can be the stillness. |

Think of the elements as stepping stones to move out of one emotional state to another. If you want to create something in your life, you need the element of fire. However, if you are stuck in your emotions (water element), you cannot create from there, unless things are flowing. You need to step into earth, get grounded or into the air element and use the breath to help you get focused and move forward.

> *'You, yourself, as much as anybody in the entire universe, deserve your love and affection.' – Buddha*

**You are who you have been looking for.** Give yourself the love you seek. Love is transformative. Look through all your fears. Look into the mirror and see that you are perfect, you are enough, you are worth it. What you say in the mirror to yourself affirms who you are becoming. Love is the answer, love is the key. How can you love someone if you cannot love yourself?

Many times, in the name of love, some of us neglect and abandon ourselves. We sacrifice and give up on our friends, family, possessions and wildest dreams. We may focus on how to keep the significant people in our lives happy so we can hold onto the relationship. Remember that the relationship that you have with yourself comes first. You matter and are worthy of your own love and respect.

---

**Daily Practice: What do I need?**

Make your own well-being a priority. Start each day with asking yourself:

What do I need to be happy today?
How can I love myself more?

---

225

## Love this moment

The lack of acceptance of the truth in the moment is what leads to a rejection of true connection to yourself. When you desire something other than what is presenting itself in this moment, you push away what you are feeling and lose your natural state of being and happiness. You push away this moment for the next. All you can do is become open, practice gratitude and love the precious moment you are in right now. When you bring your head into your heart, you will discover all is available to you in this moment.

Sometimes we only value our life when we experience a wake-up call. It could be in the form of a nightmare, a near death experience or some illness. Life takes on a different meaning and everything feels different. How will you choose to remember this time? What are you valuing about yourself and life in each moment? We learn to count our blessings and be grateful for the love in each precious moment.

> **How can you love this moment?**

# Conclusion

## Bridge Love Blueprint

If you have reached this far, congratulations for getting through all the bridges! We have one final bridge to cross and that is for you to take time out to reflect on your journey so far and create your own **Bridge Love Blueprint**. This is where you take real ownership for yourself, relationships and love life, so that you can start living an inspiractional life and love all that it has in store for you.

Once you have completed your **Bridge Love Blueprint**, it will help you to assess how far you have come since the start of your journey. It will also serve as a great reminder of the positive learnings and new discoveries you have made about yourself and your relationships. I would suggest that you put your new blueprint up somewhere where you can see it daily, and continue to practice the tools to bridge love and build new empowering ways of being.

Let's remember how far you've come. Here's a reminder of the chapters:

- Awareness Bridge

- Mindset Bridge

- Heart Bridge

- Harmony Bridge

- Communication Bridge

- Connection Bridge

- Self-Love Bridge

Look back at your notes in your journal. Take some time to review each chapter and write down what you have discovered about yourself. Which of the exercises and daily practices resonated with you? Which did you apply and how have they impacted your life and relationships? What has inspired you the most? How are you taking inspiraction?

How have you used the **Triple 'A' Formula** of awareness, acceptance and action to give you more clarity?

**Step One:**

Write down all your learnings from the **Triple 'A' Formula exercises. List your top 6 values, new empowering beliefs, new relationship codes, new stories** and any other insights you gained from the book.

**Step Two:**

Define what love means to you? Who you are becoming in love? Who are you becoming in your relationship? What is your new identity?

**Step Three:**

Write down what you need to remember and practice to ensure you are happy, loving and harmonious in love and relationships.

**Step Four:**

Take a day off either with yourself, your partner, a friend or family member and celebrate.

Ask yourself what makes you happy. Make a list of the things you love and then do them. Ask your heart what it would take to feel loved today and then go and do it, whether it is treating yourself to a pamper day, watching a movie, or taking that trip. Go out and try something completely new, exciting and adventurous that will help you get out of your comfort zone. Get in touch with the parts of yourself you have not loved enough. Forgive yourself and others for all the disappointments and unmet expectations. Treat yourself as you would treat the person you love most in your life!

We will all experience good and bad days. On the days we feel lonely and unloved, we need to acknowledge our feelings, instead of pushing them aside.

Remind yourself of the things you love about yourself. When you recognise your strengths and embrace all aspects of yourself, you feel lighter, more loved and appreciated. When the self-love fills your heart, it will spill over to your outside world. Your love will shine through in the contentment and gratitude you have for all you have gone through, all you are going through and all that you are becoming.

Decide to love yourself so fiercely that you don't need to seek any external validation to feel alive and vibrant. Choose to let go of self-defeating and limiting beliefs of separation and bask in the knowledge of oneness of all. Realise and understand that every day is and can be a celebration of life, if you gift it the presence of your attention and loving conscious care.

# Love the Journey

In conclusion, I would like to share a story of how we start as love and evolve on the relationship journey, returning to love, over and over again.

*One day we are born. We come into this world as complete and pure unconditional love, beings with bundles of energy and joy. Then life happens. We are programmed and learn to connect and relate to others – our parents, siblings, family, friends, colleagues and teachers. We may get into romantic relationships with our lovers and develop close relationships. At first these relationships seem wonderful; we feel supported, we feel loved, we feel joyous and connected.*

*Then something may happen that doesn't resonate with us. The people that we felt such a bond with are no longer the same towards us. We may leave them, or they leave our lives. We start to change and separate ourselves to create a gap and avoid feeling pain. Over time many others come into our lives and we experience that joy, love and connection again. At times we feel alone, lost and separated. We can't understand the pain and the gap gets wider as people come and people go. We realise that no one lasts forever; someday we all have to leave this world. We choose to leave some people in the past. We choose to continue walking life's path with some and keep others in our hearts, left only with precious memories of them. There may be times when we don't allow ourselves, or have the courage, to connect with another or enter into a relationship.*

*Eventually in this continuous process of coming and goings, we may lose touch with who we are. We have spent so long looking to others for the love and validation that we are seeking that we create a gap within ourselves. We start the journey again. We learn to accept, forgive others and ourselves and recognise our inner strength. We pause and learn from Mother Nature's cycles and the elements. We show ourselves compassion, heal and rise in love again. As time goes by, nothing else really seems to matter. All we are left with is ourselves. We stop judging ourselves and feeling judged. We came into this world alone and we shall go back home alone. What happens in between is a journey of discovery that takes us back to the core of our being, to embrace our true self. We learn that it was all a divine plan to realise that we were always complete, we are love, we are precious. We learn to let go of our shortfalls and re-birth ourselves. We build a bridge of love. We become more conscious and start appreciating the gift of life and connecting with others in love again. We come home to ourselves. We become love.*

*Ultimately, as humans, we are here to love one another, to co-create and bring life into the world. When we awaken to the love that is already here and become conscious in love of the behaviours and thought patterns that may be keeping us stuck, it will help us to master our relationships, break the cycle and set us free to bridge love, creating a ripple effect for future generations to come.*

**Continuing the journey and next steps**

**The journey to love takes courage, commitment, action and focus to keep going no matter what happens.**

This is not the end of the journey. It's a new beginning to continue your journey of love.

If you have enjoyed reading this book, please do share it with others. If you want to explore further, I'd like to invite you to join the **Bridge the Love Gap coaching programme**, where you will work with me at an experiential level to break through your barriers and create lasting love and connection in your life.

To learn more please **visit** my website – https://neelagohil.com

Please feel free to join and follow the fan page and become part of the community – **Neela Gohil** https://www.facebook.com/bridgethelovegap

You can also **subscribe** to my **YouTube** channel for more inspiration.

*Love your life and trust the process. Be happy and remember to have some fun along the way!*

**It's time to bridge the gap and re-awaken to love!**

A heartfelt thank you for taking the time to choose to read this book. I hope our paths cross again soon.

*With love, all is possible,*

*Neela Gohil*